TABLE OF CONTENTS

ABOUT THE AUTHORS

Chris James

Chris James serves as Greater Boston Collegiate Coordinator for the Baptist Convention of New England. He lives in Lowell, MA where he pastors Mill City Church and Christian Student Fellowship—a multi-site ministry reaching into the heart of the UMASS Lowell and the Greater Lowell communities. Chris' life passion is making disciples of college students, challenging them to see outside their own lives, and helping them to see their part in making disciples of all nations.

Chris graduated from the University of Southern Mississippi (BA in Music) and the Southern Baptist Theological Seminary (MDiv.). Recreationally, he loves to run, read—particularly theology and presidential history, and follow baseball—especially the Atlanta Braves. His recreational goal in life is to visit and watch a game at every major league ballpark (currently, he's visited 25 out of 30). You can stay connected with Chris at chrisajames.com.

Afshin Ziafat

Afshin currently resides in Frisco, Texas, with his wife Meredith and daughter Elyse. He is the Lead Pastor of Providence Church in Frisco, TX. He is also the founder of Afshin Ziafat Ministries and travels nationally and internationally proclaiming the Gospel of Jesus Christ in churches, retreats, camps, conferences, and missions. Afshin helped launch Vertical Bible Study at Baylor University in Waco, Texas. He also partners with Elam Ministries and travels into the Middle East regularly to train Iranian pastors.

Afshin's passion is to teach the Word of God as the authority and guide for life, to preach Jesus Christ as the only Savior and Redeemer of mankind, and to proclaim the love of Christ as the greatest treasure and hope in life.

Releasing Reluctance

The Mark of Millennials

Every generation is known for something.

The Builders sacrificed. The Boomers protested. Generation X questioned. Each generation is marked by sociological adjectives. Meet your generation—the Millennials. They've already carved out their generational distinctive. Among the terms used to describe them, Millennials have come to be known as noncommittal. And that noncommittal fiber is fueled by a spirit of reluctance.

According to Webster, *reluctant means* "feeling or showing aversion, hesitation, or unwillingness."[1] Millennials are inclined to display this same sense of doubt. It's a hesitancy toward almost any life commitment. It's as if they are holding out for something better while keeping all of their options open. Like it or not, this is how society views this generation. Stereotypes usually exist for a reason. But why this one?

We live in a culture that bombards us with information and opportunities. The number of options we have for education, careers, relationships, and experiences is far greater than any generation before us. At the same time, we possess a burning desire to make our lives count for something. We want life to be significant. We don't want to get it wrong. The result? Noncommitment. Hesitancy. Reluctance.

Each generation has issues to overcome, but each generation also has the hope to overcome them. The Bible tells us to be wise people and to make the most our time (see Eph. 5:15-17). Reluctance keeps you from doing that. That's why we've written *Commit*.

We want to help you release the hold reluctance has on you so you'll make wise commitments to God, His church, and to the world. Rather than holding out for something better, we want to challenge you to stick with those commitments, break the stereotypes of culture, and glorify God in the process by making your life count.

How to Use This Book

What better way to learn about commitment than in community with others? That's why we've designed *Commit* as a small-group Bible study. Geared for a no-prep small-group experience, this study is intended to be facilitator-led with a strong discussion focus. In each session you'll find:

- Questions to help you and/or your group process the Scriptures and content of each session

- Facilitator tips (*) to help effectively lead the gathering

- A "This Week Reflect On ... " section at the close of each session to allow you to reflect on what was learned and put the session into practice in your personal life

Commit to God

by Chris James

Commit your activities to the LORD,
and your plans will be achieved.

Proverbs 16:3

Commitment to God may seem like a no-brainer. After all, this is a Christian Bible study. Life characterized by total commitment to God should stand as the foundation of a Bible study on commitment. However, recent studies reveal that wholehearted commitment to God among professing Christians may not be an assumption that should be made. One study reveals 70% of students leave the church once they graduate from high school.[1] Another study shows only 51% of professing evangelical Christians consider God to be their highest priority in life.[2] There's a disconnect between what is confessed with the mouth and what is practiced in life.

List some actions or attributes that describe someone who is totally committed to God.

Would you consider yourself to be totally committed to God? Explain.

COMPARTMENTALIZING GOD

MEMORY VERSES
Psalm 73:25-26
John 17:3
Colossians 3:3-4

Do you remember the lunch trays you had in elementary school? They had nice compartments that kept all of your food in its proper place. They worked well for me. I was one of those kids who didn't want any food touching. The Salisbury steak need not touch the peas. The peas better not hop the fence into the mashed potatoes. And who wants to eat a roll doused in gravy? For kids like me, those trays were a welcomed tool for eating lunch.

Those same trays help us understand the disconnect contained in the previous statistics. Could it be that professing Christians aren't totally committed to God because they view their

*Facilitator: What truth(s) stand out to you most as you read Session 1?

lives very similarly to the food on those trays? Just as we compartmentalize lunch into different food groups, our lives are compartmentalized into different spheres. At school you're a student. At home you're a family member. At work you're an employee. At church you're a worshiper. And just like the kid who doesn't want the peas mixed with the potatoes, you keep every area of your life separated from the others as much as possible. Home doesn't touch work. Work doesn't touch school. School doesn't touch church. And church certainly doesn't touch everything else. As a result, life is comprised of a bunch of disjointed parts.

> There is no compartmentalization of the faith, no realm, no sphere, no business, no politic in which the Lordship of Christ will be excluded. We either make him Lord of all lords, or we deny him as Lord of any.[3]
>
> **–Lee Camp**

As Christians, we generally seek to resolve the commitment issue by making God the "top priority" of life (or the largest compartment on the tray). The solution, we say, is to give God priority over every other sphere of life. Or, we try to incorporate Him into each of those spheres. Consequently, we might be committed to God well in the school arena, but not so much at work. Or we are deeply committed to God at church, but not so much when hanging out with friends. This compartmentalization of life misses the mark on what total commitment to God looks like.

God doesn't desire for you to "fit Him into" every sphere of your life where total commitment to Him is distinct from the rest of your life. Scripture show us that through Christ, God is our life—the very Source from which all other spheres flow. So rather than God being the largest compartment on the tray of priorities, He instead is the tray of life where every other sphere finds its meaning and purpose.

In his letter to the church at Colossae, the apostle Paul shows us that when we give our life to Jesus, He isn't a new priority of life. Instead, He becomes our new identity.

> **For you have died, and your life is hidden with Christ in God. When Christ who is your life appears, then you also will appear with him in glory (Col. 3:3-4, ESV).**

---

* Facilitator: What does it practically look like to view God as the "tray of life where every other sphere finds its meaning and purpose"?

Read these two verses again and underline the words or phrases that communicate the truth that Jesus is the Christian's very identity.

How does knowing this truth affect the way you view commitment to God?

If you've been a Christian for any length of time, you've generally adopted a new vocabulary of phrases to communicate the change that has taken place in your life. You may be used to hearing and saying things like, "I asked Jesus into my heart," or "I walked the aisle," or "Jesus is now my personal Lord and Savior." For those who have grown up as a church kid, you may have "lettered" in Sunday School and know all six verses of "Just as I Am" by heart. Yet, when asked if you're committed to God, you draw a blank stare. Why? Often times, a chasm lies between our Christian rituals and a deep-seated devotion to God.

Throughout the rest of this session we will walk through Scripture and look at three different illustrations of total commitment to God. You'll be challenged to refrain from simply seeing God as an addition to your life and instead begin seeing Him as your all-encompassing identity through Jesus. Ultimately, you'll see that total commitment to God begins and continues in a comprehensive relationship with God.

COMPREHENSIVE DEVOTION

A total commitment to God requires comprehensive devotion. Throughout the Gospels, two groups of religious leaders repeatedly tried to trip Jesus up by questioning Him in matters of theology. The Pharisees and Sadducees knew God's law frontward and backward. They were considered to be the "religious sheriffs" of first-century Jerusalem. Although both groups were very influential and morally authoritative, they disagreed on several points of theology. And, from a sense of pride, they didn't like each other very

One of the signs that you may not grasp the unique, radical nature of the gospel is that you are certain that you do.[4]

–Timothy Keller

* Facilitator: Have someone in your group read the sidebar quote by Timothy Keller. How do you respond to Keller's point?

much either. But, in the midst of their competition for power and disagreement over theology, they were united in their dislike and jealousy of Jesus.

After Jesus left the Sadducees speechless in Matthew 22, the Pharisees tried their luck at catching Jesus using His own words. They sent one of their top-notch religious experts to go toe-to-toe with Jesus. The Scriptures recount:

> **When the Pharisees heard that He had silenced the Sadducees, they came together. And one of them, an expert in the law, asked a question to test Him: "Teacher, which command in the law is the greatest?" He said to him, "Love the Lord your God with all your heart, with all your soul, and with all your mind. This is the greatest and most important command"** (Matt. 22:34-38).

The familiar is often misunderstood.

This lawyer knew the Scriptures impeccably well. He, along with his Pharisee buddies, studied and debated about what mattered and what didn't. The scribes and Pharisees found all 613 laws from the books of Moses, and they divided them by levels of importance. If any Jewish passerby approached this guy with a question regarding morality or the law, he would quickly have an answer. Yet he still asked the question, "Teacher, which command in the law is the greatest?"

What about today? We too look for answers to life's most perplexing questions. "The Hokey Pokey—is that really what it's all about?" "How many licks does it take to get to the center of a Tootsie Pop®?" Okay, maybe those aren't that important. But real questions of life and

Aheb, the Hebrew word for love used in Deuteronomy 6:5, refers primarily to an act of mind and will, the determined care for the welfare of something or someone. It might well include strong emotion, but its distinguishing characteristics were the dedication and commitment of choice. It is the love that recognizes and chooses to follow that which is righteous, noble, and true, regardless of what one's feelings in a matter might be. It is the Hebrew equivalent of the Greek agapao in the New Testament, the verb of intelligent, purposeful, and committed love that is an act of the will. [5]

–John MacArthur

---

* Facilitator: In what ways do you feel you have to prove yourself to God?

commitment are everywhere. And just like the religious elite of Jesus' day, we also debate rituals and traditions.

"Is it more important to go to church or the campus ministry?"

"Should I go on the mission trip or go to the Christian conference?"

"It doesn't really matter what we believe if we just love each other, right?"

"Is it really important that I join a church?"

Culturally, there are many questions regarding life, religion, and God. We too argue over what's most important. We attempt to answer the only way we know how—with what we know to be normal or familiar. But the familiar is often a misunderstanding of what God has put forth in His Word.

What spiritual topics do you hear Christians in your circles debate as most important? Why do you think these topics come up often?

The problem with many of our questions is that there are many different people giving many different answers! What we're really looking for is the ultimate answer. Like this religious lawyer, we need understanding brought to our confusion. We need an ultimate interpreter of the law. That brings us to Jesus and His response to this very devoutly religious man. Again, Jesus said in verse 37:

> **Love the Lord your God with all your heart, with all your soul, and with all your mind. This is the greatest and most important command.**

A closer examination of Jesus' response reveals something that should shock those of us who are "experienced in all things Christian"—regardless of what denominational world you're coming from. Jesus gave them the most-quoted Scripture in all of Judaism. He quoted Deuteronomy 6:5—what's commonly known as the *Shema*. A devout Jew would

repeat this passage two times a day. Everyone knew this passage. Jesus basically told this man, "You do something out of religious duty and ritual on a daily basis, but totally miss the true meaning of it."

I wonder if the same could be said about believers today. Are there truths that have become so familiar that they have lost their meaning and power? Do we even know the difference between Christianese phrases and Scripture? Are you trusting so much in your religious works that you miss your spiritual devotion? The familiar is so often misunderstood.

RECOMMENDED READING
Recommended reading for seeing devotion to God as the basis of all of life:

Gospel by J.D. Greear
Gospel in Life by Timothy Keller
Spiritual Disciplines for the Christian Life by Donald Whitney
Follow Me by David Platt
His Word in My Heart by Janet Pope

What are some spiritual practices done on a regular basis you do without thinking about it?

It's what's inside that counts.

Jesus didn't respond with a list of regiments or disciplines. Instead, the greatest commandment is actually an internal state of the heart. And the heart that God looks for is personified by deep-seated devotion— devotion to Him. When Jesus said, "Love the Lord your God with all your heart, with all your soul, and with all your mind," He wasn't giving us a compartmentalized list to fit Him into. He illustrated the comprehensive nature of the devotion to Christ that's meant to envelope everything.

Bible scholar and teacher, Dr. D.A. Carson, explains devotion as this, "[These] are not mutually exclusive but overlapping categories, together demanding our love for God to come from our whole person, our every faculty and capacity."[6] In other words, there's one primary thing that serves as the lens through which we see all others. And, that primary thing is comprehensive love and devotion to God.

You don't need a change of behavior. You need a change of heart. The heart-change produces the behavior-change. In God's kingdom,

---

* Facilitator: What are some spiritual practices done on a regular basis in the church that we do without thinking about them? How would viewing life in Christ more comprehensively affect the way we do those things?

JESUS AND THE OLD TESTAMENT LAW

Jesus is the perfect
explanation of the law.

Jesus is the perfect
example of the law.

Jesus is the perfect
enabler of the law.

commitment to Him doesn't begin with the things you're supposed to do. It begins with who you're supposed to be. Doing flows from being. External behavior flows from an internal heart. Total commitment to God is always first and foremost an internal matter of the heart—a heart personified by comprehensive devotion.

UNWAVERING LOYALTY

Total commitment to God also requires unwavering loyalty. Glance through the Old Testament. God always had a people. In the Old Testament, that people was the Israelites. They were God's chosen people. He called them. He loved them. He fought for them. He delivered them. He provided for them. But they disobeyed Him. They murmured against Him. They even worshiped other gods before Him. Hit replay. The pattern continued over and over again. Same song, different verse.

During the time of the kings, many of Israel's leaders neither followed the Lord nor honored Him with their reign. King Ahab was certainly one of them. As a matter of fact, the Bible says that he "did what was evil in the LORD's sight more than all who were before him" (1 Kings 16:30). During his 22-year reign over Israel, Ahab provoked the Lord and incited the Lord's people to disobedience and idol worship. He even married a pagan idol-worshiper named Jezebel who brought her false gods into the camp of God's people. Instead of singing Yahweh's praises alone and single-heartedly praying the Shema, Israel also bowed at altars of Baal (the pagan rain god). To sum it up, the Bible says, "Ahab did more to provoke the LORD God of Israel than all the kings of Israel who were before him" (1 Kings 16:33).

Meet Elijah. One of the towering examples of faithfulness from the Old Testament, he stood as a simple yet rugged man. There was nothing flashy about him. No riches. No royalty. Just an ordinary, yet faithful man sent out to be the voice of warning to God's people against the king. Let's pick it up in 1 Kings 18:17-22:

> **When Ahab saw Elijah, Ahab said to him, "Is that you, you destroyer of Israel?"**

---

* Facilitator: Do you know someone who always seems to seek others' approval? How does that affect your relationship with them? Do you know someone who always seems to seek God's approval? How does that seem to affect their relationship with God?

He replied, "I have not destroyed Israel, but you and your father's house have, because you have abandoned the Lord's commands and followed the Baals. Now summon all Israel to meet me at Mount Carmel, along with the 450 prophets of Baal and the 400 prophets of Asherah who eat at Jezebel's table."

So Ahab summoned all the Israelites and gathered the prophets at Mount Carmel. Then Elijah approached all the people and said, "How long will you hesitate between two opinions? If Yahweh is God, follow Him. But if Baal, follow him." But the people didn't answer him a word.

Then Elijah said to the people, "I am the only remaining prophet of the Lord, but Baal's prophets are 450 men.

Describe a time you had the opportunity to take a stand for your faith and you faithfully took it.

Describe a time you had the opportunity to take a stand for your faith and you passively ignored it.

God will never tolerate a divided heart—no matter how religious you may be. Unwavering loyalty is what God demands from all who profess to follow Him. The evidence from Scripture is overwhelming:

Do not have other gods besides me (Ex. 20:3).

Therefore, fear the LORD and worship Him in sincerity and truth. Get rid of the gods your fathers worshiped beyond the Euphrates River and in Egypt, and worship Yahweh. But if it doesn't please you to worship Yahweh, choose for yourselves today the one you will worship. ... As for me and my family, we will worship Yahweh (Josh. 24:14-15).

No god was formed before Me, and there will be none after Me. I, I am Yahweh, and there is no other Savior but Me. I alone declared, saved, and proclaimed—and not some foreign god among you (Isa. 43:10b-12a).

I know your works, that you are neither cold nor hot. So, because you are lukewarm, and neither hot nor cold, I am going to vomit you out of My mouth (Rev. 3:15-16).

God continually called for unwavering loyalty throughout Scripture. Elijah trumpeted it to the wayward Israelites at Mount Carmel. Jesus repeated the same call to the church at Laodicea in the New Testament. God has never and will never tolerate a divided heart.

Don't miss the primary audience to which all of these warnings were given: the religious! The Israelites experienced first-hand the miraculous works and provision of God. They enjoyed special favor and intimacy with God, yet they still wavered. They clung to cultural idols while at the same time expressed solidarity with Yahweh. But that won't stand in God's house! In His kingdom, it's never *God and*. It's always *God alone*.

> He loves thee too little who loves anything together with thee which he loves not for thy sake.[7]
>
> **–Augustine**

So what about you? How long will you waiver? Are you expressing solidarity with God while at the same time clinging to cultural idols? Are you trying to be both a follower of Jesus and a follower of the world? Is your life during the week divorced from your worship on Sunday? Do you have one set of values with your "church" friends and another with your "worldly" friends? You'll never be totally committed to God while living on the spiritual fence. If God is God, then follow Him wholeheartedly. If not, do your own thing. That won't come without consequences, but you can't follow God and live in the middle. Partial loyalty is still complete idolatry.

What are some of the cultural idols in your life that inhibit your total commitment to God?

---

*Facilitator: From the list of Scriptures on pages 17-18, which one seems to be speaking to your heart the most right now? Why?

What is God saying to your heart about an unwavering loyalty to Him?

God always empowers a devoted heart—no matter how alone you may be. The opposite of a divided heart is a devoted heart. In the midst of disobedience, Elijah stood as a stark contrast to his Israelite brethren.

> **Then Elijah said to the people, "I am the only remaining prophet of the LORD, but Baal's prophets are 450 men" (1 Kings 18:22).**

Can you hear the valor and loyalty in his words? Elijah demonstrated courage and faithfulness in the face of unpopularity and waywardness. If you read the remainder of 1 Kings 18, you'll see how God both empowered this devoted prophet and vindicated His own glory on Mount Carmel.

The quest continues. Our Lord is still searching for people who will make a difference. Christians dare not be mediocre. We dare not dissolve into the background or blend into the neutral scenery of this world. Sometimes you have to look awfully close and talk awfully long before an individual will declare his allegiance to God. Sometimes you have to look long and hard to find someone with the courage to stand alone for God. Is that what we have created today in this age of tolerance and compromise? Elijah's life teaches us what the Lord requires.[8]

– **Charles Swindoll**

Today you may feel like the only Christian within a square mile. It could be that you're the only member of your family with a prayer life. Maybe you're the sole person in your circle of friends without a fake ID for the weekend "outings." Regardless, stand in the gap. Make hard choices. Demonstrate total commitment to God with your unwavering loyalty to Him. He always empowers a devoted heart.

In what sphere of your life do you feel most alone serving the Lord? Explain.

How does knowing that God has empowered you affect the way you view that sphere?

*Facilitator: Why is it important to recognize that so many of God's challenges in the Bible were not written to pagans but instead to the religious? Do you see any connections between Elijah's setting and ours?

RADICAL ABANDON

Finally, a total commitment to God requires radical abandon. Few places in the Bible illustrate total commitment to God like Matthew 4. The reason? When Jesus called His first disciples, their response was characterized by nothing less than radical abandon. They didn't yet understand everything He had called them to, but they literally left everything they knew and had to obey the commands of Jesus.

> How important that we revel in and understand and experience the love of God and, in the power and assurance of that love, declare it to the world.[9]
>
> **– Dave Hunt**

As He was walking along the Sea of Galilee, He saw two brothers, Simon, who was called Peter, and his brother Andrew. They were casting a net into the sea, since they were fishermen. "Follow Me," He told them, "and I will make you fish for people!" Immediately they left their nets and followed Him.

Going on from there, He saw two other brothers, James the son of Zebedee, and his brother John. They were in a boat with Zebedee their father, mending their nets, and He called them. Immediately they left the boat and their father and followed Him (Matt. 4:18-22).

Those first disciples taught us what happens when Jesus bids us come: we leave behind all things in order to live for one thing.[10]

We leave behind all things

These men were fishermen by trade. This was a family business. Children didn't have the opportunity to go away in order to "find themselves" at Nazareth College or Jerusalem State. They usually did what their father did. Fishing was all they knew and it was all they were expected to do.

Moreover, family served as the epicenter of Jewish culture. You were to respect your father. The bond one had with their father because of cultural lineage customs even trumped the marital bond in many cases. That's why Matthew 4 is so noteworthy. Matthew 4:22 says they "immediately they left the boat and their father and followed Him." They walked off the job. They left their dad. When Jesus spoke, they left behind everything they knew to follow Him.

Jesus' expectations are no less radical today, but you wouldn't know it by examining churches today. Our obsession with education, careers, riches, family, reputation, recreation, comfort, and safety should cause us to stop and think. Have you truly abandoned it all to follow Jesus? Or are you simply trying to fit Jesus into a life you've created for yourself? A life totally committed to God is the life that is radically abandoned to Jesus. It's a life that has counted the cost and left behind all things.

How does the radical testimony of the first disciples differ from your understanding of what it means to follow Jesus?

What specific thing is most difficult for you to imagine "leaving behind" for the sake of following Jesus?

We live for one thing—to follow Jesus.
What made those fishermen make such a radical life decision? You or I could say, "abandon it all to follow me" and receive a room full of blank stares. But Jesus makes demands and the response is radical abandon. The gravity of the command has everything to do with the person making it. When Jesus speaks people leave everything behind and live for one thing. Now, this doesn't mean that all of those things we obsess over are evil in and of

Nobody stood and applauded them

So they knew from the start
This road would not lead to fame

All they really knew for sure was
Jesus had called to them

He said "Come follow me"
and they came

With reckless abandon they came

Empty nets lying there at the
water's edge

Told a story that few could
believe and none could explain

How some crazy fishermen agreed
to go where Jesus led

With no thought for what they
would gain

For Jesus had called them by
name and they answered

We will abandon it all for the
sake of the call

No other reason at all but the
sake of the call

Wholly devoted to live and to die

For the sake of the call [11]

"For the Sake of the Call"

– Steven Curtis Chapman

themselves. As a matter of fact, many of those things are precious gifts of God when viewed the right way. But when we come face-to-face with the commands of Jesus, we find something worth losing everything for and Someone worth surrendering everything to.[12] That one thing is the gospel of Jesus Christ. And that Someone is Jesus Christ.

Our response to Jesus must be more than just walking down an aisle or asking Him into our hearts. An obedient response to Jesus must include a change in worldview—we need to see life through a brand new set of lenses. As a result, we ask how our careers, possessions, relationships, and everything else can be leveraged for the sake of knowing Jesus and making Him known. Consequently, areas of life become an extension of the rule and reign of Christ.

J.D. Greear communicates it this way:

> **The gospel is not just supposed to be our ticket into heaven; it is to be an entirely new basis for how we relate to God, ourselves, and others. It is to be the source from which everything else flows.[13]**

This worldview shift stands as the basis of a life totally committed to God and changes everything. God is no longer a separate compartment in your life—now everything in your life finds meaning and purpose from your commitment to God. The gospel is not only the means through which we are saved, but also the power from which we live and the identity to which we hold. Commitment to God isn't something you work up enough effort to will on your own. It's this same gospel that fuels comprehensive devotion, unwavering loyalty, and radical abandon to God. So the very characteristics of the total commitment God requires, He Himself gives through Jesus Christ.

How is the Holy Spirit changing how you think about relating to God and what total commitment to Him looks like?

---

* Facilitator: What would it look like for young adults to leave behind all things in order to follow Jesus like the first-century disciples? What stands in the way of getting there?

THIS WEEK REFLECT ON…

GROWING WITH GOD

There is a common characteristic personifying the heroes of the faith who were totally committed to God (like Elijah and the disciples): when they truly encountered the God of the universe, their lives were radically changed. Take a moment to examine your heart through prayer by asking the question, "Have I truly encountered God and seen Him for who He is within the Scriptures?" Perhaps you need to commit yourself to reading Scripture as you seek to live totally committed to God. Or maybe you need to abandon everything to follow Jesus with your life.

MAKING A CHANGE

Begin reading Scripture systematically to be exposed to "the whole counsel of God" (Acts 20:27). This includes:

- Reading the Bible book-by-book
- Reading longer portions at a time (3-4 chapters)
- Reading repetitively (staying in the same book for a week or two)

For example, Philippians contains four chapters. Perhaps you could read the entire Book of Philippians every day for a week. Or, Matthew contains 28 chapters. You could read four chapters per day for a week and go through the entire book.

Incorporate prayer into your times of Scripture reading. Ask God to give you understanding, nourish your soul, and reveal Himself to you through those times.

FURTHER STUDY

For an in-depth look at understanding and applying the gospel to your life, check out *Engage* (available at *threadsmedia.com*).

Commit to the Church

by Afshin Ziafat

[The] church is not a place. It's not a building.
It's not a preaching point. It's not a spiritual
service provider. It's a people—the new
covenant, blood-bought people of God.[1]

–Mark Dever

I loved everything about collegiate life. My days in college were the most formative in my journey with Christ and understanding the calling He placed on my life. This is probably why college students are some of my favorite people to minister to.

Over the years, I've heard two common complaints about college students. The first is that many Christian high school graduates move away to college and subsequently drift away from the Lord. The second complaint is that college students spend the majority of their Sundays "church hopping." They don't commit to one local church in their college town, but rather hop around to various church services. I believe these two complaints are closely related. Why? I believe the reason many college students drift away from the Lord is because they don't commit to a local expression of God's church.

The truth is, God created us for community. But more than that, those who have come to saving faith in Christ have also been *saved* for community. Scripture teaches us that the second we become Christians, we're adopted by God. We're called "children of God" (1 John 3:1, ESV). God becomes our Father through faith in Jesus Christ, and other believers become our siblings in Christ. This is why 1 John 3 goes on to say that if we don't love our brother in times of need, then we are questioned on whether we truly have the love of God in us (see 1 John 3:16-18). Therefore, a commitment to God is truly made manifest through a commitment to God's family—the church.

How would you respond to the previous statement, that a commitment to God is truly made manifest through a commitment to the church?

Our aim in this session is to see how God has always called His people to Himself to live in community and advance His mission in the world. We'll see that the church is the people of God among whom Christ dwells today. A true Christ follower is committed to Christ's church. And finally, we'll see the importance of faithful membership to a local church, especially during your college years. Let's get started!

MEMORY VERSES
Hebrews 10:25
Ephesians 2:19-22
Ephesians 4:12-16

A BIBLICAL HISTORY OF GOD'S PEOPLE

The apostle Paul wrote to the church at Ephesus that "Christ loved the church and gave Himself up for her" (Eph. 5:25). The term *church* is used to apply to all those whom Christ died to redeem. Jesus' death is the means by which both Old Testament and New Testament believers are saved, whether they looked forward to the cross or looked back at the finished work of Christ on the cross. Even in the Old Testament God thought of His people as a *church*—a people assembled for the worship of God. Deuteronomy 4:10 says, "Assemble the people before Me, and I will let them hear My words, so that they may learn to fear Me all the days they live on the earth and may instruct their children." In the Greek translation of the Old Testament, the root of the word rendered *assemble* is the same word that is used for the church (*ekklesia*). In Acts 7:38, Stephen referred to the people of Israel as the church or congregation in the wilderness. Therefore we see the church as the people of God all throughout Scripture.

> The church is the community of all true believers for all time.[2]
>
> – **Wayne Grudem**

How do you respond to the idea that you're a part of a people that has been gathering together, worshiping, and serving the same God, well before the coming of Christ?

Why do you think the concept of community is given so much attention in Scripture, both in the Old Testament and New Testament?

Throughout redemptive history, God created a people where His presence dwelled and He was reflected to the world. In the creation account, God spoke creation and man into being. God created Adam and said that it wasn't good for man to be alone, and He created Eve (see Gen. 2:18). Scripture says God created male and female in His own image (see Gen. 1:27).

God is a triune God, meaning Father, Son, and Holy Spirit are together in perfect, selfless community. Therefore God created humans for

---

* Facilitator: What truths stand out to you in this session? Why?

RUTH'S COMMITMENT TO NAOMI

During the time of the judges, there was a famine in the land. ... Naomi was left without her two children and without her husband. She and her daughters-in-law prepared to leave the land of Moab, because she had heard in Moab that the Lord had paid attention to His people's need by providing them food. ... She said to them, "Each of you go back to your mother's home. May the Lord show faithful love to you as you have shown to the dead and to me. May the Lord enable each of you to find security in the house of your new husband." She kissed them, and they wept loudly. "No," they said to her. "We will go with you to your people." But Naomi replied, "Return home, my daughters. Why do you want to go with me? Am I able to have any more sons who could become your husbands? Return home, my daughters." ... Orpah kissed her mother-in-law, but Ruth clung to her. Naomi said, "Look, your sister-in-law has gone back to her people and to her god. Follow your sister-in-law." But Ruth replied: Do not persuade me to leave you or go back and not follow you. For wherever you go, I will go, and wherever you live, I will live; your people will be my people, and your God will be my God. Where you die, I will die, and there I will be buried. May Yahweh punish me, and do so severely, if anything but death separates you and me (Ruth 1:1-17).

community. Adam and Eve lived in perfect communion with God and each other in the garden of Eden. God's presence was among them and they reflected God's being to the world.

However, things didn't stay this way. Adam and Eve disobeyed God and ate from the one tree from which they were forbidden to eat (see Gen. 2:17; 3:6-7). Immediately their relationship with God and each other was broken. Sin drove them to hide from God, and Adam blamed Eve for his own sin. They were both driven from the garden and out of God's presence (see Gen. 3:7-24). They were still image bearers of God, but that image was now corrupted by sin.

How have you seen sin damage relationships in your life? How have you seen sin damage community within the church?

Adam and Eve disobeyed God's Word. Community was broken, they were driven out of God's presence, and they no longer reflected God like they once did. But even in the garden, God gave a glimpse of how He would restore His presence among His people and reflect His nature through the church. God made a promise that the future offspring of Eve would crush the serpent that brought sin into the world, and this would lead to mankind's reconciliation with God (see Gen. 3:14-16).

God's plan of reconciliation began with His calling of Abraham in Genesis 12. God told Abraham that He would create a nation through him. They would be His people, and He would be their God. He would dwell among them, and through

---

* Facilitator: What does Scripture mean when it says man was created in God's image (see Gen. 1:27)?

Abraham and his offspring, God promised to bless all the families of the earth (see Gen. 12:1-3). Again we see God created a collective people, not just individuals. His presence would be with these people, and they would reflect Him to the world. This is what Israel was to be.

Years later, God redeemed His people out of the bondage of slavery in Egypt through the leadership of Moses (see Ex. 14). God gathered His people at Mount Sinai and gave them His law (see Ex. 31–32). By keeping the law, the people of God would reflect Him to the world around them. As they were led through the wilderness, God's presence was with them in the tabernacle.

And finally, Joshua led God's people into the promised land (see Josh. 1–5), and years later, Solomon built the temple (see 1 Kings 6). God's people were in God's land with God's presence among them. They were to be a light to all the Gentile world.

But time and time again, God's people rebelled against Him. They were driven out of God's presence into exile. The Old Testament closed with the people of God in the promised land, longing for God to return to His temple. But for 400 years, God did not speak to His people until He ultimately spoke to them in His perfect revelation—Jesus, the Word made flesh.

Is it helpful to understand commitment to the church in light of this history of God's people? Why or why not?

GOD'S PEOPLE TODAY—THE CHURCH

We've taken a quick ride through the Old Testament to discover the establishment of God's people through Abraham. In the New Testament, though, we get a fuller vision for God's purpose for His people in the coming of His Son. Through Jesus, God created a new people who would be in His presence and reflect His glory to the world. Through Jesus, the New Testament church was birthed.

Let's begin by looking at John 2. Here we find the popular story of Jesus driving all the money changers out of the temple. The Jews asked Him

---

* Facilitator: Did humanity lose the image of God after the fall?

what authority He had. Jesus replied, "Destroy this sanctuary, and I will raise it up in three days" (John 2:19). The Jews didn't understand that Jesus would rise from the dead three days after His crucifixion. Through His death and resurrection, Jesus created a new temple where God's presence would dwell—the church. The gospel gives birth to the church.

In 1 Peter we learn that we have been born again of an imperishable seed "through the living and enduring word of God" (1 Pet. 1:23). Peter continued to write, "This is the word that was preached as the gospel to you" (1 Pet. 1:25). Once again we see that the gospel gives birth to spiritual life. But it doesn't just give birth to an individual life—it gives birth to a corporate body.

In 1 Peter 2 we learn that those who have been born again are like living stones, being built up as a spiritual house. The purpose? To be a holy priesthood and offer spiritual sacrifices through Jesus Christ who is the "chosen and honored cornerstone" of this new house (see 1 Pet. 2:5-6). Believers in Christ make up the new temple and become a holy priesthood. In the Old Testament times, only the high priest could enter the presence of God and offer sacrifices. But now, because we have a Great High Priest in Jesus, we can boldly approach the presence of God through Him (see Heb. 4:14-16). So what we see here is the corporate community of believers—the church—is where the presence of God dwells. First Peter 2:9 gives us the nature and purpose of the church.

> Local church membership is a question of biblical obedience, not personal preference.[3]
>
> **– Matt Chandler**

> **But you are a chosen race, a royal priesthood, a holy nation, a people for His possession, so that you may proclaim the praises of the One who called you out of darkness into His marvelous light.**

God has made us His people for the express purpose of declaring His excellencies and reflecting His glory to the world.

You would probably place great value in declaring God's excellencies and reflecting His glory on an individual level, but what kind of value do you place on these things while being united with other believers?

The beauty of the gospel is that through the sacrifice of Christ, sinful humans can be reconciled to a holy God and to one another! Unison to God in Christ yields the fruit of unison with every Christian.

In Ephesians 2, Paul wrote that both Jews and Gentiles have access to the Father through Christ and that the two are made one in Christ.

> So then you are no longer foreigners and strangers, but fellow citizens with the saints, and members of God's household, built on the foundation of the apostles and prophets, with Christ Jesus Himself as the cornerstone. The whole building, being put together by Him, grows into a holy sanctuary in the Lord. You also are being built together for God's dwelling in the Spirit (Eph. 2:19-22).

Why is it significant that both Jews and Gentiles have access to the Father through Christ?

> God did not give us the local church to become country clubs where membership means we have privileges and perks. He placed us in churches to serve, to care for others, to pray for leaders, to learn, to teach, to give, and, in some cases, to die for the sake of the gospel. Many churches are weak because we have members who have turned the meaning of membership upside down. It's time to get it right. It's time to become a church member as God intended. It's time to give instead of being entitled.[4]
>
> – Thom Rainer

As Paul progressed through this passage, he intensified the intimacy of Christians with one another. He moved from saying believers are "fellow citizens," and proceeded to say they were "members of God's household" (v. 19). The apostle continued to say that believers are built together to form a "holy sanctuary" (v. 21).

This is similar to the intensifying relationship between my wife and me. Because my family emigrated from Iran before I was born, I was born as an American citizen—the same citizenship as my wife. When I became a Christian, I became a member of the same spiritual family as my wife, who accepted Christ a couple of years before me. When we married, we became one in Christ through marriage. Though this isn't a perfect analogy, it speaks to the depth of unity that believers should have. As fellow bricks that are joined together to build the house of God, we're dependent upon one another.

---

* Facilitator: When you hear the word *church*, what comes to mind? How would define what a church is?

COMMIT TO THE LOCAL CHURCH

All of this brings us to the question of why this is relevant for us today. You may ask, "If we are part of the universal church (the collection of all believers), then why is there a need to commit to the local church (a smaller group of believers that meet in a specific area)? Where does the Bible say I need to become a member of a church?"

Local churches and church membership is addressed throughout the New Testament. The epistles, in fact, are addressed to local churches. For example, the Book of 1 Corinthians starts with an address to "God's church at Corinth" (1 Cor. 1:2).

Local church membership is also implied in the New Testament passages encouraging church discipline. In 2 Corinthians 5, Paul urged the Corinthian church to "put away the evil person from among yourselves" (v. 13). And in Matthew 18, Jesus exhorted the church to regard the expelled person as a pagan. Both of these commands are dependent upon a clear distinction between who is and isn't a part of the local body.

Furthermore, the fact that local church leadership is clearly mandated underscores the necessity for there to be an identifiable church membership. Hebrews 13:17 says,

> Obey your leaders and submit to them, for they keep watch over your souls as those who will give an account, so that they can do this with joy and not with grief, for that would be unprofitable for you.

In 1 Peter, we see elders are urged to shepherd their flocks, all the while looking to Jesus, the chief Shepherd (see 1 Pet. 5:2-4). Commandments like these would be difficult for church leaders to follow if they didn't know the exact flock they were held accountable to. It's clear in Scripture that a Christian needs to be a member of a local church.

Has there been a time in your life when you've been content only being a part of the universal church and not committing to the local church? If yes, what was the appeal?

---

* Facilitator: Why is corporate worship so important?

Now that we have seen the strong implication in Scripture for local church membership, it's important for us to see the many benefits of belonging to a local church. I'll give you eight, but know there are many more I don't have the space to mention.

THE IMPORTANCE OF CHURCH MEMBERSHIP

1) It's how God primarily shepherds your soul.

Psalms 23 and 100 taught every Jew to view their relationship with God in a unique way. The Hebrew people were God's chosen people and God was their Shepherd. God shepherded His people through judges He put in place to govern His people. But when the leaders of Israel didn't properly care for God's people, God promised He would shepherd His people Himself (see Ezek. 34). This was a foreshadowing of Jesus and His ministry. In John 10:11, Jesus said to His listeners, "I am the good shepherd. The good shepherd lays down his life for the sheep." Jesus shepherded His 12 disciples by teaching them that the Son of Man came not to be served, but to serve and give His life as a ransom for many (see Mark 10:45). After His resurrection, Jesus commanded His disciple Peter to tend and feed His sheep (see John 21:15-16). It's this same Peter who exhorted his fellow elders to shepherd their flocks in 1 Peter 5.

It's clear that God has always intended for His sheep to be led by shepherds. Jesus is the chief Shepherd who calls and prepares men as undershepherds to lead His church. In fact, these undershepherds or pastors are God's primary means of shepherding His church. This is how God guides, protects, leads, and restores the souls of His people.

> One of the great things about living as part of a community is that in community people walk all over your idols. People press your buttons. That's when we respond with bitterness, rage, and so on. And that gives us opportunities to spot our idolatrous desires.[5]
>
> **– Tim Chester**

> You and I cannot demonstrate love or joy or peace or patience or kindness sitting all by ourselves on an island. No, we demonstrate it when the people we have committed to loving give us good reasons not to love them, but we do anyway.[6]
>
> **– Mark Dever**

---

* Facilitator: In what ways does church membership differ from other forms of membership?

Have you experienced this kind of shepherding within the church? How important is it for you to have mentors or leaders in the church speaking into your life?

2) It's where sanctification takes place.

God's intent is for everyone who comes to faith in Christ to grow in Christlikeness as they follow Him through life. God intended this sanctifying work to take place through the context of community. Since the garden of Eden, sin has tempted mankind to withdraw into darkness and isolation. When Adam and Eve first sinned, they not only attempted to cover themselves, but they also tried to hide from God's presence. Read what Jesus had to say in John 3:19-20.

> This, then, is the judgment: The light has come into the world, and people loved darkness rather than the light because their deeds were evil. For everyone who practices wicked things hates the light and avoids it, so that his deeds may not be exposed.

We're all sinners. Our flesh will always pull us toward isolation and away from the light, where our sins can be exposed. Scripture is clear that the only way to walk in the light is in community.

> But if we walk in the light as He Himself is in the light, we have fellowship with one another, and the blood of Jesus His Son cleanses us from all sin (1 John 1:7).

Walking in the light means to walk in fellowship with other believers. However, it's important to note that many people think they're walking in fellowship, but it's not the kind of authentic community John referred to in his first epistle. John continued by writing,

> If we say, "We have no sin," we are deceiving ourselves, and the truth is not in us. If we confess our sins, He is faithful and righteous to forgive us our sins and to cleanse us from all unrighteousness. If we say, "We don't have any sin," we make Him a liar, and His word is not in us (1 John 1:8-10).

So the kind of fellowship that will sanctify us is fellowship that's transparent and authentic, where sin isn't covered up but confessed openly. Being a committed member to a local church forces us to walk alongside people who know our sins, struggles, and fears and can truly hold us accountable.

Is this concept of community scary to you—one where sins, struggles, and fears are in the open? Why or why not?

> …even if your function in the body of Christ is that of a pinky toe, you will be sorely missed, because you are needed for proper functioning of the body.[7]
>
> – C. Michael Patton

What are the potential benefits to this kind of openness within community?

Church community not only helps a Christians defeat sin in his or her life, but it's also the arena where spiritual maturity occurs. Consider the fruits of the Spirit listed in the Book of Galatians.

> **But the fruit of the Spirit is love, joy, peace, patience, kindness, goodness, faith, gentleness, self-control. Against such things there is no law (Gal. 5:22-23).**

Most of the these fruits are only relevant within the context of community. These fruits are only seen and developed relationally. One doesn't grow in love, patience, kindness, goodness, faithfulness, and gentleness in seclusion, but rather in fellowship with others as we learn to extend these Spirit-filled virtues toward one another.

Because of the fall, the image of God created in mankind has been marred by sin. But Christ's work of sanctification through the Holy Spirit is to restore that image to followers of Christ. In the Book of Colossians, Paul said that followers of Christ are to put off the old self and put on the new self—the one that is being renewed in the image of its Creator.

---

* Facilitator: How do you think God might be using other people to bear more fruit of the Spirit? How do you think He might be using you to do the same in others?

> Therefore, God's chosen ones, holy and loved, put on heartfelt compassion, kindness, humility, gentleness, and patience, accepting one another and forgiving one another if anyone has a complaint against another. Just as the Lord has forgiven you, so you must also forgive. Above all, put on love—the perfect bond of unity (Col. 3:12-14).

Again we see a list of qualities that reflect the image of God—qualities that are only instilled in the Christian through the context of community. This list in Colossians assumes conflict will happen. But conflict is when most people jump ship and leave the church. When this happens, the work of sanctification is short-circuited. We need to be committed to the church because we need to be sanctified.

3) It's how our gifts are identified and where our gifts are to be employed. The great significance of Christ's resurrection and ascension is that those who put faith in His finished work of redemption can find justification and eternal life. However, Scripture teaches us that along with those great benefits, we also receive spiritual gifts because He has ascended (see Eph. 4:7-8). We also know that everyone who God calls to Himself receives gifts that are unique to Him.

> Now as we have many parts in one body, and all the parts do not have the same function, in the same way we who are many are one body in Christ and individually members of one another. According to the grace given to us, we have different gifts (Rom. 12:4-6a).

These gifts aren't given to us for our own edification but for the strengthening of the church.

> Now there are different gifts, but the same Spirit. There are different ministries, but the same Lord. And there are different activities, but the same God activates each gift in each person. A demonstration of the Spirit is given to each person to produce what is beneficial (1 Cor. 12:4-7).

Paul equated church members with members of a physical body. He stated that all parts of the body—the eye, the foot, the hand—are

necessary and play a significant role in the body. Furthermore all parts of the body are dependent on one another. So the gifts are ultimately not for the individual but for the church! Therefore it stands to reason that it's only in the confines of the church that your gifts can be identified.

How have you seen this kind of collaboration play out in the church—members using individual gifts to accomplish one goal and purpose?

Many times I've received emails from young men who aspire to preach, either as an itinerant evangelist (which I was for many years) or as a pastor (which I am today). I always tell them to start in the local church where they belong. It's there that your gifts are nurtured. It's there that your gifts are confirmed by others in the body. As a young believer I began sharing my testimony and teaching God's Word in my local church's Sunday school classes. Many church members began to tell me they saw a gifting on my life for teaching and preaching.

> No one is meant to walk alone in the Christian life. The New Testament makes this clear through its repeated emphasis on "one another" commandments:
>
> Romans 12:10,16
> Romans 14:13,19
> Romans 15:7,14
> Galatians 5:13
> Galatians 6:2
> Ephesians 5:21
> Ephesians 4:32
> Philippians 2:3
> Colossians 3:9,13,16
> 1 Thessalonians 3:12
> 1 Thessalonians 4:18
> 1 Thessalonians 5:11,13
> Hebrews 10:24
> James 5:16
> 1 John 1:7

Furthermore, the church is where God trains and instills in you the qualities necessary for future ministry. Long before David was the king and shepherd of God's people, he shepherded his father's flock faithfully. Long before David killed Goliath, he fought off the lion and bear in the field with his father's flock. Jesus taught that one who is faithful in the little will be faithful in much (see Luke 16:10). Local church membership is key to discovering the gifts the Lord has entrusted to you.

4) It's how the church is built up.
The reason our gifts are to be employed within the church is also because this is God's means of building up His church. A church's health is proportionate to the number of members who have discovered their gifts and are using them for the building of the body.

And He personally gave some to be apostles, some prophets, some evangelists, some pastors and teachers, for the training of the saints in the work of ministry, to build up the body of Christ, until we all reach unity in the faith and in the knowledge of God's Son, growing into a mature man with a stature measured by Christ's fullness. Then we will no longer be little children, tossed by the waves and blown around by every wind of teaching, by human cunning with cleverness in the techniques of deceit. But speaking the truth in love, let us grow in every way into Him who is the head—Christ. From Him the whole body, fitted and knit together by every supporting ligament, promotes the growth of the body for building up itself in love by the proper working of each individual part (Eph. 4:11-16).

In this passage we see that the role of church leaders is to equip the saints for the work of ministry. Most people falsely believe that the work of ministry is restricted to pastors or church staff. But this text shows us that every member is a minister. Furthermore, the church will grow strong and resist the Devil's schemes when every saint of the church is using their gifts. Church isn't just a place where you sing songs, hear a sermon, and meet fellow believers. Church is where you find your place to use your gifts to grow the body of Christ to maturity. Being committed to the church is fundamental to being engaged in God's ultimate plan of making disciples—the growth and expansion of the church.

How important is it for you personally to be connected to the church through your service, disciple-making, and the expansion of your church's vision?

5) It's where our calling is affirmed.

Not only are our gifts identified in the local church, but our calling is confirmed there as well. For example, everyone knows about the missionary exploits of the apostle Paul that are recorded in the Book of Acts. But Paul didn't just decide by himself that he would become a missionary for Jesus. In Acts 9 the Lord drew Paul to saving faith and

called him to carry His name to the Gentiles. But many overlook the fact that Paul's calling was confirmed by a local church and its elders. Yes, Paul was a faithful member of a local church, using his gifts to build up the church before he was sent out to do missionary work. In Acts 11, we see that Saul (Paul's Hebrew name) was with Barnabas teaching the Word of God in the church at Antioch (see Acts 11:25-26). In Acts 13, we learn that the church was gathered together with its leaders in worship and fasting. This is where calling was confirmed and affirmed by the Holy Spirit and the church.

> As they were ministering to the Lord and fasting, the Holy Spirit said, "Set apart for Me Barnabas and Saul for the work I have called them to." Then after they had fasted, prayed, and laid hands on them, they sent them off (Acts 13:2-3).

In the church, non-Christians should see the kind of unity and love that testifies to the truth and power of the gospel and God's love (John 13:34-35; 17:20-21). Our friends will see the gospel with their eyes as they witness Christians observing baptism and the Lord's Supper. Both in the way we live together as a church and in the ordinances of the church, we display the gospel in ways that complement the preached word of the gospel.[8]

– Thabiti Anyabwile

Even at the end of their missionary journey, we see that Paul and Barnabas returned to their church in Antioch to report all that God had done with them (see Acts 14:26-28). The apostle Paul didn't receive and engage in his calling separately from the life of the local church.

6) It's how you keep an eternal perspective.

Of utmost importance to the Christian life is a keen awareness that we're just passing through this world, and our hope and destination is the eternal kingdom of God. Repeatedly throughout Scripture we see commands to invest in eternity instead of clinging to this world. We're told not to store up treasures here on earth (see Matt. 6:19); to not put our trust in riches but in God who richly provides (see 1 Tim. 6:17); to wait on Jesus who will deliver us from the wrath to come (see 1 Thess. 1:10); to hasten the day of the Lord because we know that all earthly things will be dissolved (see 2 Pet. 3:12). It's easy to lose focus on this reality and get swept up in the temporary things of this world. This is why the church is essential to maintaining a proper eternal perspective in life. We need other believers as examples of what it looks like to run after the eternal.

> Join in imitating me, brothers, and observe those who live according to the example you have in us. For I have often told you, and now say again with tears, that many live as enemies of the cross of Christ. Their end is destruction; their god is their stomach; their glory is in their shame. They are focused on earthly things, but our citizenship is in heaven, from which we also eagerly wait for a Savior, the Lord Jesus Christ (Phil. 3:17-20).

Give a few examples of accountability you've received because of your commitment to the church.

Are you being reminded of the gospel and the hope you have in Christ? If not, whom within the church can you seek out to receive this kind of constant eternal perspective?

This is why we gather in church. Scripture is clear when we live separate from the life of the church, we'll lose perspective on our eternal hope.

> Let us hold on to the confession of our hope without wavering, for He who promised is faithful. And let us be concerned about one another in order to promote love and good works, not staying away from our worship meetings, as some habitually do, but encouraging each other, and all the more as you see the day drawing near (Heb. 10:23-25)

7) It's where we find comfort in trials.
Scripture assures us that trials will come, suffering is to be expected, and God is good even in the midst of tribulations.

Read Romans 8:28-39 and briefly describe how this passage speaks to God's love in the midst of trial.

_____

Suffering isn't merely a possible experience we may walk through but an eventual and certain reality we all must face in life. But God hasn't left you alone to deal with it and He hasn't purposed suffering in your life without reason. God uses trials to shape us to be more complete.

> **Consider it a great joy, my brothers, whenever you experience various trials, knowing that the testing of your faith produces endurance. But endurance must do its complete work, so that you may be mature and complete, lacking nothing (Jas. 1:2-4).**

Trials are not just meant to equip the individual Christian but the entire church. The church is where you can endure suffering in life, and it's where your suffering finds purpose.

> **Praise the God and Father of our Lord Jesus Christ, the Father of mercies and the God of all comfort. He comforts us in all our affliction, so that we may be able to comfort those who are in any kind of affliction, through the comfort we ourselves receive from God. For as the sufferings of Christ overflow to us, so through Christ our comfort also overflows. If we are afflicted, it is for your comfort and salvation. If we are comforted, it is for your comfort, which is experienced in your endurance of the same sufferings that we suffer. And our hope for you is firm, because we know that as you share in the sufferings, so you will share in the comfort (2 Cor. 1:3-7).**

We see here that God uses the church to comfort us so that we can turn around and comfort others with the love and support we have received. So the church isn't only how we are comforted but how our suffering finds purpose. If you suffer in isolation, you waste a key aspect of suffering's intention—to build up and encourage others.

8) It's how Christ is reflected to the world.

In John 17, Jesus prayed that the future church would be one just as He and the Father are one. He prayed for this unity so that the world would know that He had been sent (see John 17:20-21). Our triune God is One of selfless unity. The Father glorifies the Son, the Son glorifies the Father,

the Spirit glorifies the Son, etc. When the church displays selfless unity, the world can see the God we worship.

Paul urged the Philippian church to be in full accord and one mind. He commanded them to count others more significant than themselves and to put the interests of others before their own. Then he gave them the ultimate reason for this: it reflects the way Christ selflessly loved us to the point of the cross (see Phil. 2:1-11). It is impossible to display this selfless unity of the Lord unless you're a committed member of a local church.

Jesus is also reflected to the world when we truly love other members of the body of Christ. He did this by loving us and laying His life down for us. His desire is that we would do the same for one another.

> This is My command: Love one another as I have loved you. No one has greater love than this, that someone would lay down his life for his friends (John 15:12-13).

The greatest news in the world is that God's love for us wasn't something we earned, but that He loved us while we were His enemies (see Rom. 5:8). This is the message the world desperately needs to hear. Most world religions teach that you have to love God enough so that He will love you. But only in Christianity do you have the message that we love God because He first loved us (see 1 John 4:19). When members of the church love one another unconditionally, Christ Himself is made manifest to the world. If we love one another, God abides in us and His love is perfected in us (see 1 John 4:12).

> What God did to us, we then owed to others. The more we received, the more we were able to give.[9]
>
> – Dietrich Bonhoeffer

Once again, it's impossible to fulfill this calling of reflecting Christ to the world apart from the church. It's impossible to love in isolation. In fact, the distinguishing characteristic of a Christian is love. Therefore local church involvement is an indispensable part of the Christian life.

> I give you a new command: Love one another. Just as I have loved you, you must also love one another. By this all people will know that you are My disciples, if you have love for one another (John 13:34-35).

---

* **Facilitator:** In what ways have you seen the difficulties of community in your own life?

THIS WEEK REFLECT ON…

GROWING WITH GOD

Reread and reflect on the "Ruth's Commitment to Naomi" sidebar on page 32. What stands out to you the most in this passage? How can this story apply to our commitment to God's people in the local church?

Also, spend some time reading through the story of Nehemiah. This book of the Bible details a story of great commitment to God's people. Nehemiah turned down a position next to the King of Persia to return to his people in order to help them rebuild the city walls of Jerusalem. The Jews accomplished their goal despite great opposition.

MAKING A CHANGE

Look over the eight important reasons why you should be a church member. Determine the two or three areas where you need the people of the church to speak into your life. You may need to give comfort or receive comfort because of a trial. You may have noticed God given gifts that need to be employed in the church. You may also need someone within the church body to mentor you on a specific area of sin within your life. Circle the areas below and take action.

1) It's how God primarily shepherds your soul.
2) It's where sanctification takes place.
3) It's how our gifts are identified and where our gifts are to be employed.
4) It's how the church is built up.
5) It's where our calling is affirmed.
6) It's how you keep an eternal perspective
7) It's where we find comfort in trials.
8) It's how Christ is reflected to the world.

If you aren't connected to a church, commit to finding one where you can serve, give financially, invest your time and energy, and make disciples.

FURTHER STUDY

If you want to know more about being actively committed to the church, consider the following resources.

- *Mentor* by Chuck Lawless (available at *threadsmedia.com*)
- *The Millennials* by Thom Rainer and Jess Rainer
- *I Am a Church Member* by Thom Rainer

Commit to the World

by Chris James

The driving force [for missions] is love—love for God and love for others. Having been loved and redeemed, the proper response of those who know Christ is to want others to benefit from the infinite measure of that same love.[1]

–David Horner

When Jesus told His disciples, "Love the Lord your God with all your heart, with all your soul, and with all your mind" (Matt. 22:37), He was describing what total commitment to God looks like—comprehensive devotion. Accompanying that devotion to God is a commitment to people: "Love your neighbor as yourself" (Matt. 22:39). This neighborly love means deep-seated, brotherly affection for God's people (the church). But love for the brethren must not remain dormant. It influences. It expands. Therefore, total commitment to God and total commitment to His people propels us into a new-found commitment to those in the world.

YOUR DILEMMA

An interesting dichotomy stares us in the face here in the second decade of the twenty-first century. On one hand, there's no shortage of need in the world. The homeless walk our cities' streets. Our neighbors are unchurched. Orphans wait for parents. Women and children are sold into sexual slavery. Villages drink disease-infested water. Earthquakes and tsunamis devastate regions. Christians die for their faith. And entire people groups have absolutely no access to the gospel.

The Western church, on the other hand, is extremely blessed. We're safe. We have lavish resources. We're deeply educated. We have access to what seems like unlimited information. As a matter of fact, college students in America know more about global realities than any generation before them. In this wealthy information age, the world is smaller than it has ever been; the church has more resources than ever before; and we know more about the needs of the world than we've ever known. Yet all of those needs in the world remain.

MEMORY VERSES
Micah 6:8
Matthew 5:13-16
Ephesians 2:10

When you hear about all of the areas of global need, what moves you to compassion the most? Why?

When thinking about love and commitment to the people of the world, there could be one of several different responses to these realities mentioned. As a young adult, you may be reluctant to get involved for numerous reasons:

* Facilitator: What truths stand out to you most in this session? Why?

- **Ignorance:** You're unaware.
- **Indifference:** You don't care.
- **Individualism:** You have your own needs to take care of.
- **Passivity:** You assume someone else will take care of it.
- **Guilt:** You wish you didn't have so much.
- **Caution:** You don't think you can make a difference.
- **Confusion:** You have no idea where to begin.
- **Anxiety:** You think you're responsible to do it all.

From this list of responses, which one(s) describes your reluctance most? Why?

Your generation is passionate about justice for many things. Aids in Africa. Sex-trafficking. Corporate greed. Poverty. And thanks to social media, multiple platforms exist to channel that passion and advocacy. In addition, concerts and conferences fill your calendars where almost every artist introduces you to yet another way to serve others in Jesus' name. But advocacy and information doesn't automatically equate action and relief.

But your generation is also one of action. You sincerely want to make a difference. You watch your peers serve meals to the homeless. They build houses with Habitat for Humanity. They give money to drill water wells. They volunteer in after-school programs. Yet sometimes you're still overwhelmed at the need and even confused about where to begin.

There are many different ways to help meet the needs of the world. But could the barrage of opportunities and awareness available to us actually debilitate us in our response? Do all of our options leave us immobile as we wrestle with indecision of where to begin? Are we mistaking social awareness for actual social justice? Are we involved in so many causes that we aren't very good at any? Do we know the difference between "making disciples of all nations" and providing for "the least of these"? And because very few of us experience the ills ourselves, do we debate the problems more than we actually deliver solutions?

These questions stand at the very heart of the issue of commitment. It's one thing to be committed in principle. It's another thing altogether to be committed in practice. It's one thing to Tweet about the number of orphans in the world. It's quite another to pray for them on a consistent basis. It might be easier to sing about missions at a conference than to make the sacrifices necessary to be on mission in the world. For many of us, being committed to the world sounds more like an ideal to hold onto rather than a life that can really be lived out. After all, there are so many people with so many needs and so many organizations working to address them. You might ask, "How do I even start?" I'm so glad you asked.

YOUR RESPONSE

How do you release your reluctance of committing to the world? Regardless of where you find yourself on that list of improper responses, I propose a different response. A response that moves the passive to action and directs the overzealous and worn out to a clearer focus. A response that addresses the needs of the world and is worthy of following Jesus. Here it is: Know that God calls you to missional action, but He doesn't call you to do it all. Look in the first chapter of Mark how Jesus, in order to stay focused on His mission, intentionally didn't attempt to do it all.

> When evening came, after the sun had set, they began bringing to Him all those who were sick and those who were demon-possessed. The whole town was assembled at the door, and He healed many who were sick with various diseases and drove out many demons. But He would not permit the demons to speak, because they knew Him.
>
> Very early in the morning, while it was still dark, He got up, went out, and made His way to a deserted place. And He was praying there. Simon and his companions went searching for Him. They found Him and said, "Everyone's looking for You!"
>
> And He said to them, "Let's go on to the neighboring villages so that I may preach there too. This is why I have come." So He went into all of Galilee, preaching in their synagogues and driving out demons (Mark 1:32-39).

* Facilitator: Do you think the barrage of opportunities and awareness available to us today debilitates us in our response? Why or why not?

What types of ministry was Jesus doing?

Do you find the conclusion odd? Why or why not?

Jesus left town and left needy people standing in line. Sounds crazy, right? But it's true. Why? Why would the Savior of the world who also "loved the world" (John 3:16) live this way? Because the focus of His mission was clear. He knew what He was sent to do—to seek and to save that which was lost. Therefore He confidently stayed on track throughout His earthly ministry.

What if you lived with a laser-focus similar to Jesus? What if your passionate generation of action could channel its spiritual energy in such a way that the mission of each person was characterized by focused commitment rather than fuzzy advocacy? In other words, what if you committed your life to a few people or a single ministry rather than attempting to conquer world hunger, open an adoption agency, and translate the Bible in 12 languages all before lunch on Friday?

Your temptation might be to read this chapter and hear, "More, more, more! There's so much need. So little time. Step it up. Get working. Vámanos!" But that's not the goal. Instead, focus your spiritual energy and gifts in the right direction. Stop simply talking about the problems. Refrain from hiding behind social media. Cease attempting to do it all. Because in trying to commit to everything, you really commit to nothing. Maybe what you need is a challenge to do something of real missional significance.

---

* Facilitator: What is the difference between focused commitment and fuzzy advocacy? What would it look like to commit your life to a few people or a single ministry instead of giving very little energy to many things?

Have you ever stopped to think that maybe Jesus is not calling you to do more, but instead something of real missional significance?

What do you think this may look like for you?

YOUR CALLING

The Bible repeatedly illustrates the influence God's people are to have on the world around them.

> So we must not get tired of doing good, for we will reap at the proper time if we don't give up. Therefore, as we have opportunity, we must work for the good of all, especially for those who belong to the household of faith (Gal. 6:9-10).

> For we are His creation, created in Christ Jesus for good works (Eph. 2:10).

> He gave Himself for us to redeem us from all lawlessness and to cleanse for Himself a people for His own possession, eager to do good works (Titus 2:14).

What common theme do you hear when reading through the above passages? Go back through these texts underlining that theme.

---

* Facilitator: Why is it so important do good works as a result of salvation rather than doing good works to achieve salvation?

Get the picture? As a follower of Christ, your calling is to live in such a way that marks you as belonging to Him. A crucial distinction must be made here. You were not saved *by* producing good works. You were saved *to* produce good works. First comes new life. Then comes the works. To get these out of order is to miss the heart of the gospel altogether. The fruit of your forgiveness is influence—upon both the church and the world.

But part of your reluctance to commit to something or someone might lie in the flood of options and need. Maybe you're saying, "I'm all about doing good works, but for what am I responsible? How do I know where to begin?"

The answer is partially found in Galatians 6:10 in the phrase, "as we have opportunity." These words signify that we're personally responsible for some needs more than others—particularly those right in front of us. It's what some have called "moral proximity"—the closer the need, the greater the moral obligation to help. God will hold us personally accountable more for the needy family across the street than the homeless family in Africa. And we're more personally responsible for a family member in Europe than a stranger in Asia. This proximity includes both geography and relationship.

Moral proximity gives us a starting point regarding commitment to the world. But we can't stop there because we know Jesus has sent us into the whole world (see John 17:18; 20:21). When Jesus gave His mission to the disciples, it was to start locally and expand globally. It's difficult to care about the hungry child in Africa if you don't possess concern for your lost roommate. Commit yourself to those needs in your immediate circles first. Then allow that concern to expand even to the ends of the earth.

For the remainder of our time, let's flesh out this idea more specifically. What does it look like to live out this calling of producing "good works"?

1. Commit yourself to the unassuming.

In America, very few expect anyone to do anything good toward them. Whether it's your roommate, a family member, or a stranger on the street, our culture says, "I'm all set. I can make it on my own." People assume little. They expect nothing. So when a Christian does random acts of kindness or goes the extra mile, it immediately causes most to pause and reflect. This is what is meant by serving the unassuming.

JEWS AND SAMARITANS

In the days of Christ, the relationship between Jews and the Samaritans was greatly strained. The animosity was so great that the Jews bypassed Samaria as they traveled between Galilee and Judea. They went an extra distance through the barren land Perea on the eastern side of the Jordan to avoid going through Samaria. Yet Jesus rebuked His disciples for their hostility to the Samaritans (Luke 9:55-56), healed a Samaritan leper (Luke 17:16), honored a Samaritan for his neighborliness (Luke 10:30-37), asked a drink from a Samaritan woman (John 4:7), and preached to the Samaritans (John 4:40-42). Then in Acts 1:8, Jesus challenged His disciples to witness in Samaria. Philip, a deacon, opened a mission in Samaria (Acts 8:5). A small Samaritan community continues to this day to follow the traditional worship near Schechem.[4]

Describe a time when someone took you by surprise and served you in a random, yet meaningful way. How did you respond?

In Luke 10:30-37, Jesus delivered a memorable parable and illustrated the importance of serving other people.

Jesus took up the question and said: "A man was going down from Jerusalem to Jericho and fell into the hands of robbers. They stripped him, beat him up, and fled, leaving him half dead. A priest happened to be going down that road. When he saw him, he passed by on the other side. In the same way, a Levite, when he arrived at the place and saw him, passed by on the other side. But a Samaritan on his journey came up to him, and when he saw the man, he had compassion. He went over to him and bandaged his wounds, pouring on olive oil and wine. Then he put him on his own animal, brought him to an inn, and took care of him. The next day he took out two denarii, gave them to the innkeeper, and said, 'Take care of him. When I come back I'll reimburse you for whatever extra you spend.'

"Which of these three do you think proved to be a neighbor to the man who fell into the hands of the robbers?"
"The one who showed mercy to him," he said.

Then Jesus told him, "Go and do the same."

By reading this parable now, we lack the insight that reveals the scandalous nature of Jesus' illustration to this primarily Jewish audience. The Samaritans were the mixed-breed race resulting from the Jews' intermarrying with pagans during the Babylonian captivity. Consequently, the Samaritan people were constant objects of derision and prejudice from the Jews. Imagine the sting that came when Jesus painted a Samaritan as the hero of His story on neighborly love, especially when He was connecting neighborly love and devotion to God (see Luke 10:25-29)!

Jesus also calls us to this same type of sacrificial service toward our neighbors. It may not always be providing a hospital stay for a stranger lying in a ditch, but radical commitment through sacrificial service should personify all believers in Jesus. And it should begin with the unassuming in our immediate circles.

In the same way, let your light shine before men, so that they may see your good works and give glory to your Father in heaven (Matt. 5:16).

From Jesus' standpoint, there lies a connection between believers' good works and nonbelievers' view of God. In living out your calling to display good works, begin with the unassuming in your immediate sphere of influence. Always be ready to serve others in Jesus' name in practical ways. Then expand that influence throughout your city and wherever you go.

Maybe it could look something like this:

- Serve your roommate by cleaning up his or her mess.
- Make cookies for the residents in your dorm during final exams.
- Get permission from your university for your campus ministry to distribute free packs of

For more great ideas on serving your community through random acts of kindness, see *101 Ways to Reach your Community* by Steve Sjogren.

[A] major effect that the gospel of grace has on a person is that it creates spontaneous generosity. The priest and the Levite did not stop despite biblical injunctions to help a countryman. But no one expects the Samaritan to give mercy. One of the reasons that Jesus puts a Samaritan in the story is that he, by virtue of his race and history, has no obligations at all to stop and give aid. No law, no social convention, no religious prescription dictates that he render service. Yet he stops. Why? … He was moved by his compassion.[4]

– Timothy Keller

---

* Facilitator: Brainstorm some practical ways that your group could commit to the unassuming on your campus or in your community.

gum with a simple business card that says, "This is a random act of kindness to show you the love of Jesus in a tangible way." Include your ministry's contact information.

- Shovel your neighbor's driveway after a winter snow or rake your neighbor's autumn leaves with no expectation of payment.

What are some additional ways you could commit to the unassuming in your spheres of influence (at home, work, school, or in your community)?

These acts might not always be well received by the unassuming around you. It may be a little unnerving to you when you first begin. But know that God has called you to do good works in the world, beginning with those in closest proximity to you.

2. Commit yourself to the unloved.

Social justice is a popular topic among both Christians and non-Christians; it's where many people find common ground, regardless of political views. And rightly so. It's hard to imagine being against helping people affected by homelessness, sex-trafficking, or poverty. In recent years, a plethora of information regarding these plights has come to our attention, largely because of social media. What once may have been out of sight and out of mind to other generations is now right within your grasp.

But increased information shouldn't lead us to conclude that these things are new or that our advocacy is somehow a recent trend. Biblical mandates from thousands of years ago command Christians to provide relief for the unloved of the world.

> Wash yourselves. Cleanse yourselves. Remove your evil deeds from My sight. Stop doing evil. Learn to do what is good. Seek justice. Correct the oppressor. Defend the rights of the fatherless. Plead the widow's cause (Isa. 1:16-17).

> **He has told you, O man, what is good; and what does the LORD require of you but to do justice, and to love kindness, and to walk humbly with your God?** (Mic. 6:8, ESV)

> **Pure and undefiled religion before our God and Father is this: to look after orphans and widows in their distress and to keep oneself unstained by the world** (Jas. 1:27)

History tells us that the early church followed God's commands. The Greco-Roman world suffered several plagues and epidemics in the third and fourth centuries. One historian and sociologist traced how the Christians' reaction to the plagues differed dramatically from that of those who maintained faith in traditional, polytheistic paganism. Roman Emperor Julian was quoted as saying, "The impious Galileans [Christians] support not only their poor, but ours as well, everyone can see that our people lack aid from us."[5]

We're going to look at some ways to follow the example of those early Christians. But, first, let's address two types of people. The first is the student who takes on every injustice as a personal project and frowns upon anyone who doesn't show the same level of compassion. For this person, providing relief to victims of social injustice equates the work of the gospel. To this person, it's the ultimate mission of the church.

WHAT ABOUT JUSTICE?

Justice, as a biblical category, is not synonymous with anything and everything we feel would be good for the world. We are often told that creation care is a justice issue, the gap between rich and poor is a justice issue, advocating for a "living wage" is a justice issue... but justice is a much more prosaic category in the Bible. Doing justice means not showing partiality, not stealing, not swindling, not taking advantage of the weak because they are too uninformed or unconnected to stop you. We dare say that most Christians in America are not guilty of these sorts of injustices, nor should they be made to feel that they are. We are not interested in people feeling bad just to feel bad, or worse, people thinking there is moral high ground in professing most loudly how bad they feel about themselves. If we are guilty of injustice individually or collectively, let us be rebuked in the strongest terms. By the same token, if we are guilty of hoarding our resources and failing to show generosity, then let us repent, receive forgiveness, and change. But when it comes to doing good in our communities and in the world, let's not turn every possibility into a responsibility and every opportunity into an ought. If we want to see our brothers and sisters do more for the poor and the afflicted, we'll go farther and be on safer ground if we use grace as our motivating principle instead of guilt.[5]

---

* Facilitator: Read the sidebar on social justice. How do you respond to this?

THE GREAT COMMISSION

One command:

Make disciples of all nations.

Three principles:

Intentionally pursue them (Go).

Baptize them.

Teach them.

One promise:

Jesus will always be with you.

The second dismisses social justice as a whole in exchange for the preaching of the gospel. For this person, providing relief to physical needs is futile without offering hope for ultimate spiritual needs. So who's right?

Which side of the spectrum (social justice vs. gospel mission) do you gravitate toward most often?

In essence, both sides have holes. Yes, the Scriptures command Christians to care about and offer relief from earthly oppression. But that care and concern can never substitute for the gospel-work of the heart. The work of the gospel is ultimate. But, in God's kingdom, Christ followers aren't called to preach the gospel while dismissing real human need.

As seen in the previous verses, Scripture gives commands regarding widows, orphans, people who are oppressed, and those who can't defend themselves. Although Christians may differ in their solutions or personal involvement in these issues, Scripture doesn't give us the option of being disengaged toward the unloved. Therefore, we must release our reluctance toward committing to them. But what can you do right now where you are?

- Give a restaurant gift card to the homeless.
- Spend time with senior citizens in your church—particularly those who are sick and alone.
- Frequently visit a local nursing home in order to read Scripture and pray with patients.
- Pray for the approximately 150 million orphans in the world.
- Sponsor a child in need across the globe through reputable relief organizations.
- If you plan on having a family, pray toward the possibility of one day adopting orphaned children.

---

* **Facilitator:** Brainstorm some practical ways that your group could commit to the unloved in your community or around the globe.

- Visit relevant websites that detail global oppression (including famine, the sex trade, and orphan-care).
- If God has given you great concern for the sick and oppressed, explore opportunities to move to another part of the world to be the hands and feet of Jesus.

3. Commit yourself to the unengaged. God has called us to live a life of influence. That influence is evidenced by doing good works toward the unassuming and providing relief to the unloved. But each of these commitments serve only as a part of the Christian's commitment to the world. The heart of Christ's mission to the world is what we know as the Great Commission.

> Missions is not the ultimate goal of the church. Worship is. Missions exists because worship doesn't. Worship is ultimate, not missions, because God is ultimate, not man. When this age is over, and the countless millions of the redeemed fall on their faces before the throne of God, missions will be no more. It is a temporary necessity. But worship abides forever.
>
> Worship, therefore, is the fuel and goal of missions. It's the goal of missions because in missions we simply aim to bring the nations into the white-hot enjoyment of God's glory. The goal of missions is the gladness of the peoples in the greatness of God.[6]
>
> **– John Piper**

> Then Jesus came near and said to them, "All authority has been given to Me in heaven and on earth. Go, therefore, and make disciples of all nations, baptizing them in the name of the Father and of the Son and of the Holy Spirit, teaching them to observe everything I have commanded you. And remember, I am with you always, to the end of the age" (Matt. 28:18-20).

In the muddied waters of Christian action, we live in a day where everything is mission. Doing good works is mission. Relieving the poor is mission. Stopping the sex-trade is mission. But when Jesus gave His parting commands to the disciples, He defined the ultimate mission of the church: to make disciples of all nations. The phrase Jesus used is "make disciples of *panta ta ethne*"—literally every tribe or ethnicity on earth. So in a world where everything can be called mission, guard yourself from confusion. If everything is mission, nothing is mission.

---

*Facilitator: If Piper is right that worship is the ultimate goal of the church, then why does it only make sense that making disciples be the ultimate mission of the church?

Why is it important to remember the ultimate mission of the church?

How do you respond to the statement, "If everything is mission, nothing is mission"?

Jesus commanded His followers to "make disciples of all nations." Today, missiologists divide the nations into people groups. Recent statistics shows there are more than 16,000 people groups in the world and nearly 7,000 of those groups are considered *unreached*.[7] This means there is no indigenous community of believing Christians with adequate numbers and resources to evangelize their people. The term *unengaged* is also used to describe people groups who have no mission strategy to reach them.

We live in a lost world—one that is very much unengaged in regard to the gospel of Jesus Christ. Whether it's your roommate on the other side of the room, your foreign neighbor on the other side of the street, or the people group on the other side of the globe, God commands His people to make disciples of all nations.

And it all starts right where you are—among your sphere of influence. Then it spreads. It starts locally. It expands globally. Jesus said as much to His disciples.

For more information about committing to the unengaged, check out these resources:

Operation World: The Definitive Prayer Guide to Every Nation by Jason Mandryk

www.radical.net

www.joshuproject.net

www.imbstudents.org

But you will receive power when the Holy Spirit has come on you, and you will be My witnesses in Jerusalem, in all Judea and Samaria, and to the ends of the earth (Acts 1:8).

The staggering statistics of a world unengaged from the gospel may leave you overwhelmed and even reluctant to begin. But Jesus had a firm strategy. His intent was for each of His followers to personally commit to a small number of people for the sake of the gospel. That's what He meant when He commanded them to "make disciples." Disciples are made, and that requires time, commitment, and energy. The goal is to invest and teach in such a way that the disciples you are making become disciple-makers themselves. In his book, *The Master Plan of Evangelism*, Robert Coleman gives this helpful insight.

> We should not expect a great number to begin with, nor should we desire it. The best work is always done with a few. Better to give a year or so to one or two people who learn what it means to conquer for Christ than to spend a lifetime with a congregation just keeping the program going. Nor does it matter how small or inauspicious the beginning may be; what counts is that those to whom we do give priority in our life learn to give it away.[8]

It's time to release your hold on reluctance. If the gospel is to spread globally, it will be because it took root locally. The missionaries of greatest influence started with making disciples in their personal sphere of influence. Commit yourself to the unengaged. Know that your local obedience means global impact. As pastor and author David Platt has said, "We are the plan of God, and there is no Plan B."[9] Begin God's global domino-affect today. Unreached people groups are waiting. How can you begin tackling the task of engaging the unengaged?

- Begin by learning about and praying for the world. The resources in the sidebar on page 62 are great tools to get you started.
- Initiate a conversation with an unbeliever in your circle of friends. Invite him or her to read through the Gospel of John with you.
- Sacrificially give your money to the church and global mission partnerships—no matter how little you make.

- Serve on a short-term mission trip with your church or campus ministry. The first step may be the toughest, but there will be great reward in your risk.
- If you are passionate about global disciple-making, visit *www.imbstudents.org* for different mission projects.

These ideas can get you started. What are some additional ways you could commit to the unengaged in your spheres of influence or across the globe?

God intends for His people to be a people of influence. Godly influence isn't marked merely by advocacy, Facebook posts, Tweets, and debates. It's marked by commitment and action. Sometimes that action is doing good works toward our neighbors with no expectation of return. Other times, we love the unloved by giving real provision to real needs, whether the opportunity to share the gospel exists or not. At all times, we advance the ultimate mission of the church by making disciples of all nations. We serve this way knowing that individually we can't do it all. But by God's grace, we can do something of real missional significance because we invest a lot in a few rather than very little in a lot.

What has God taught you in this session?

What action steps might you take in response?

THIS WEEK REFLECT ON …

GROWING WITH GOD

Go back and look at the sidebar entitled "Jews and Samaritans" on page 56. Read the passages illustrating Jesus' commitment to the Samaritans (a very unloved people group). Pray for a heart that loves the unloved like Jesus did.

MAKING A CHANGE

If you aren't a locally-minded Christian, it will be harder to be a globally-minded Christian. Go back and review some of the good works and random acts of kindness you could demonstrate to your immediate neighbors. Strategically think about ways you may serve your family, roommates, co-workers, or local strangers. Then discuss with your Bible study group or campus ministry how to serve the people of your campus and community in creative and meaningful ways. Very few of us naturally live this way. It requires intentionality.

As you take risks locally, pray for a renewed mind globally. Ask God to give you a heart and vision to commit to the unloved and unengaged throughout the world.

FOR FURTHER STUDY

If you want to take the next steps in becoming actively committed to the people around you and the people around the world, consider the following resources.
- *Radical* by David Platt
- *Crazy Love* by Francis Chan
- *Operation World* by Jason Mandryk

Commit to Now

by Chris James

"Resolved, that I will live so, as I shall wish I had done
to die."[1]

– Jonathan Edwards

"Most people don't expect you to understand what we're going to tell you in this book. And even if you understand, they don't expect you to care. And even if you care, they don't expect you to do anything about it. And even if you do something about it, they don't expect it to last. Well, we do."[2]

If it's true that your generation doesn't commit to anything, Alex and Brett Harris didn't get the memo. The above paragraph stands as the opening lines of the twin brothers' 240-page manifesto, *Do Hard Things*, that fights against the low expectations of teenagers and young adults in America. And get this—they wrote it as 19-year-old college students! They have since traveled around the country on a crusade challenging their generation to live lives of action and commitment.

As we conclude *Commit*, our call to you is the same. We believe you're better than the low expectations that have been placed on you. We stand confident that you were created by God to live for significance. But to get there, you must release the hold reluctance has on you. And you have to break the stereotypes of hesitancy and indecision for which your generation has come to be known. Real commitments must be made to God, to His church, to your relationships, to your career, and to your mission. You don't have to wait until you graduate. You don't have to kick the proverbial can down the road. You need to begin right now, right where you are.

Where are you most paralyzed with indecision right now?

What do you think it will take to move you forward with confidence?

LIVING FOR THE DASH

Every tombstone has two dates—a birthdate and a deathdate separated by a dash. That dash represents your life. So, what are you doing with the dash? What opportunities fill the moments of your days? How will those moments define your life?

Solomon sobers us with a similar reminder:

> It is better to go to a house of mourning than to go to a house of feasting, since that is the end of all mankind, and the living should take it to heart (Eccl. 7:2).

Solomon's point? If you want to know how a person truly lived, it's better to go to his funeral than his birthday party. Humanity reflects on life the most when life ceases to exist. Take this to heart and consider your life. Live in such a way that at the end of your life you have no regrets. Jonathan Edwards echoed this truth in his famous resolutions: "Resolved, that I will live so, as I shall wish I had done when I come to die."[4]

Throughout the Bible, God tells us that our lives matter, but our lives are also short. We must make the most of every opportunity. Consider the following Scriptures.

> Teach us to number our days carefully so that we may develop wisdom in our hearts (Ps. 90:12).

> Pay careful attention, then, to how you walk—not as unwise people but as wise—making the most of the time, because the days are evil (Eph. 5:15-16).

> Act wisely toward outsiders, making the most of the time (Col. 4:5).

---

* Facilitator: What truths stand out to you most from this session? Why?

Two themes are evident in these Scriptures.

1. Make the most of the time. What this means is to make the best possible use of all circumstances. The Greek word for time, *kairos*, means *the right moment*, which Paul urged his readers to grasp lest it be wasted. A lifetime is comprised of individual moments and opportunities. And an examination of the present and the future reveals to us that the only one we're promised is the present—right now. So if you want to get to the end of your life with fewer regrets, make the most of the opportunities before you today.

But understand that hesitancy won't get you there. It's better to take risks, make mistakes, experience victories, and learn from them all than to play it safe in a constant haze of indecision. The former guarantees growth and maturity. The latter characterizes your life as a career of almosts, could have beens, and missed opportunities. So make the most of every opportunity. To do so, you must release the hold of reluctance.

> Suppose that we allot ourselves a generous eight hours a day for sleep (and few need more than that), three hours for meals and conversation, ten hours for work and travel on five days. Still we have thirty-five hours each week to fill. What happens to them? How are they invested? A person's entire contribution to the kingdom of God may turn on how those hours are used. Certainly those hours determine whether life is commonplace or extraordinary.[5]
>
> – J. Oswald Sanders

If someone wrote a biography of your life, what would you want them to say characterizes your life?

What would they actually say characterizes your life?

2. Walk in wisdom. Wisdom is one of the most important qualities of godly living. Wisdom can be defined as the ability to discern right from wrong based on the revelation of God in the Scriptures. According to the aforementioned passages, there's a connection between making the most of every

---

* Facilitator: Spend some time discussing the difference between what we "want people to say about our lives" and "what actually characterizes our lives." How do we reconcile the two?

opportunity and possessing godly wisdom. A contributing factor to your hesitancy in life and commitment might be a wisdom-deficiency in your heart. But there are ways to change that.

> More than 40 percent of adult Millennials currently have a mentor in their lives.[6]
>
> **–Thom Rainer**

There are two primary ways to grow in biblical wisdom. One, commit yourself to know the Word of God. Two, commit yourself to godly mentors who can aid you in knowing and applying the Word of God to your life. These two principles, coupled with prayer, are foundational to making the most of the time that you have.

Do you have a mentor in your life whom you meet with regularly? If so, in what areas has he/she helped you most?

If not, who are some good candidates in your life who could serve you in this way?

Live for the dash by making the most of right now—live in a God-honoring way today so you have fewer regrets tomorrow. We want to empower you to release the hold of reluctance so that you truly begin to live your life right now rather than holding out for something better tomorrow. In order to do that, however, you must overcome some key contributors to reluctance's hold.

RELUCTANCE BASED UPON DISAPPOINTMENTS OF THE PAST

Could it be that you're in a virtual holding pattern of life due to disappointments or failures in your past? Maybe it's the brokenness of your own sinful choices. It could be the regrets of squandered opportunities. It might stem from your upbringing. These disappointments of the past

---

*Facilitator: Ask your group to share about significant mentors from their lives. Talk about the specific ways they have helped you apply the Word of God to your life and aided you in growing in godly wisdom.

Many reading these lines may be experiencing grief for wasted years. Despite how you may have misused your time in the past, you can improve the time that remains. The will of God for you now is found in the words of the Apostle Paul: "Forgetting what is behind and straining toward what is ahead, I press on toward the goal to win the prize for which God has called me heavenward in Christ Jesus (Philippians 3:13-14). Through the work of Christ to repentant believers, God is willing to forgive every millisecond of misused time in the past. And it is pleasing to Him for you to discipline the balance of your time for the purpose of Godliness.[7]

– Donald Whitney

accuse you while reminding you of the broken person you are. They lead you to conclude, "What does it matter anyway? Regardless of what I do, I'll never be any good."

Therefore, reluctance continues its hold. But it doesn't have to—the lies of the past can't overcome the reality of biblical truth. The Bible is full of examples of God transforming our present by redeeming our past. This reality is the whole hope in the power of the gospel of Jesus Christ.

Therefore, if anyone is in Christ, there is a new creation; old things have passed away, and look, new things have come (2 Cor. 5:17).

Brothers, I do not consider myself to have taken hold of it. But one thing I do: Forgetting what is behind and reaching forward to what is ahead, I pursue as my goal the prize promised by God's heavenly call in Christ Jesus (Phil. 3:13-14).

These scriptural truths become even more relevant when knowing their author. The apostle Paul possessed all credibility in writing about jaded pasts. He murdered Christians in the name of honoring God. Paul was actually on his way to murder more Christians when Christ appeared to him! He was what we might call a "repeat offender." But God transformed this religious zealot into the New Testament's greatest missionary. That's the power of the gospel. If God redeemed the past of Paul, how much more can He redeem yours?

In what ways are you allowing the disappointments of your past to immobilize you from moving forward?

There is no amount of disappointment, shame, or regret in your past that guarantees defeat for the rest of your life. Conversely, there is no amount of blessing, care, or victory that guarantees success for life. We are each responsible for today. So whether you grew up in privilege or poverty, success or regret, move on and release the hold of reluctance.

RELUCTANCE BASED UPON DISCONTENTMENT IN THE PRESENT
Could it be that the flood of opportunities and choices available to you inhibit you from committing to right now? Might your endless selection of choices fuel discontentment in your heart? It's hard to really commit to anything because something better may be coming down the road, right? The new job seems awesome until a help-wanted sign hangs in front of your favorite store. That major seemed like the right one until you changed it—for the third time. And you know that the iPhone® 10 is going to be so much better than the 8 or the 9 (just wait, they're coming).

This barrage of choices fuels your discontentment. These choices also debilitate you in your ability to commit; because they promise you that something better will be right around the corner. This contributes to your generation's propensity of "holding out for the next best thing." You want to keep all of your options open because something better is probably coming. So in waiting for the best thing in the future, you ultimately choose no thing in the present.

But this stands in stark contrast to who God desires you to be.

> Only let each person lead the life that the Lord has assigned to him, and to which God has called him. This is my rule in all the churches (1 Cor. 7:17, ESV).

I don't say this out of need, for I have learned to be content in whatever circumstances I am (Phil. 4:11).

God desires His people to be content. This doesn't mean you shouldn't have goals or aspire to be better. What it does mean, though, is that you must guard yourself from focusing so much on *what might be* that you miss out on *what is right in front of you.*

In what ways are you dreaming about "what could be" down the road?

Jesus loves faith-filled risk for the glory of God.[8]

– John Piper

If you're going to release the hold of reluctance on your life, you must overcome the disappointments of your past as well as the discontentment in the present. But you must also run away from distrust of the future.

RELUCTANCE BASED UPON DISTRUST OF THE FUTURE

Today more options exist for you regarding education, career, relationships, and experiences than for any generation before you. You possess a burning desire to make your life significantly count, and you don't want to get it wrong. You might be hesitant to committing to life's decisions due to distrusting the future. You're afraid of messing it up.

Many people are fearful of making wrong decisions and distorting God's entire plan for their lives. Many people—especially young adults—believe God has mapped out every twist and turn of their lives like a game board. Every decision they make is another roll of the dice. And if they make the wrong decision, there's no way to win the game. But this is an unhealthy understanding of God's will and plan for your life. The Bible doesn't reveal a turn-by-turn plan that must be individually discovered. Instead, more often than not, God asks us to be faithful with what we've been given and honor Him with what we do.

---

*Facilitator: Why does the flood of opportunities available to us fuel so much discontentment within us?

> Therefore, whether you eat or drink, or whatever you do, do everything for God's glory (1 Cor. 10:31).

> And whatever you do, in word or in deed, do everything in the name of the Lord Jesus, giving thanks to God the Father through Him (Col. 3:17).

Then, through prayer and wisdom from others, we do the next thing. The Bible gives far more instruction on how to live today than how to discover the plans for tomorrow. Even Jesus calls our attention away from placing too much emphasis on the future.

> Therefore don't worry about tomorrow, because tomorrow will worry about itself. Each day has enough trouble of its own (Matt. 6:34).

Now this doesn't minimize the gravity some decisions have. It does safeguard us, though, from overthinking or over-spiritualizing our lives. God has given us wisdom, His Word, and the Holy Spirit. With these divine resources in our grasp, God gives us great freedom and ability to make decisions of life. We actually honor God by making them. God isn't glorified in fear-based hesitancy, but instead He is glorified in wisdom-filled action. So overcome reluctance based upon distrust of the future.

Where is it most difficult to trust God with your future?

Where is reluctance's strongest hold on you? Is it the disappointments of the past, the discontentment of the present, or the distrust of the future? Why?

---

*Facilitator: Among your group, talk about how you each answered the question, "Where is reluctance's strongest hold on you?" In what ways might you encourage one another to release that hold and move forward?

HOW CAN YOU DEMONSTRATE COMMITMENT RIGHT NOW?

For the remainder of our time, let's flesh this out a little more deeply. Here are five specific ways you can release the hold of reluctance and begin demonstrating commitment right now.

1. Commit to your work.

As a pastor to college students and young adults, I often hear a response similar to this in regard to work, "Well, this is what I'm doing right now, but it's not what I really want to do."

Then, there are the cries from culture like this one, "I have $100,000 in student loans and a degree from Northeastern University. I deserve a high-paying job."

And in Thom Rainer's well-researched work, *The Millennials: Connecting to America's Largest Generation*, he references a young woman named Debbie who desires flexibility and a lavish lifestyle.

> I went straight to grad school after I got my college degree," Debbie told us. She is a twenty-four-year-old MBA student from the Chicago area. "I really don't care much about the prestige of an MBA. That's no big deal to me. What I want is the kind of job where I can have a decent living that will give me some flexibility. I really want to have the time and means to travel and visit my family. I may be unrealistic, but I don't want to wait ten or twenty years before I'm in a good financial position with a good job.[9]

Which of the above attitudes toward work and career are closest to your own? Why?

Regardless of where you will be in five years or what you hope to do in ten years, you live in your current season right at this moment. More than likely you're a full or part-time college student who also works a full or

---

* Facilitator: Who would you say is your "closest" friend? What has contributed to that closeness? Share about a time you experienced conflict, but grew through forgiveness and patience.

part-time job. It might be at a bank, but it also might be at a pizza joint. Because you view your employment as a temporary necessity for long-term purposes, you might blow off your responsibilities as a student or as a delivery boy because it's not what you "really want to do."

> **Whatever you do, do it enthusiastically, as something done for the Lord and not for men (Col. 3:23).**

God is more concerned about *how* you work than what your work is or how much your work pays you. Therefore, wholeheartedly commit to your job during this season of life. Count money, deliver pizzas, and write research papers for the glory of God. You'll cultivate a holy attitude toward work that will accompany you for life and you'll honor God in the process.

How does your attitude toward work need to change?

2. Commit to your friends.

Culture teaches you that friendship is great—until that friend hurts you, wrongs you, or betrays you. Friends who get the most attention are the friends who do the most for you. But the Bible's teaching on friendship differs greatly from the expendable view of the world.

> **No one has greater love than this, that someone would lay down his life for his friends (John 15:13).**

Jesus tells us that the apex of human love and commitment is illustrated in sacrificial friendships between His followers. As a result, we should constantly look out not only for our own interests but also for the interests of our friends (see Phil. 2:4).

We also must demonstrate forgiveness and patience when someone has wronged us. When Paul told the Ephesians to "bear with one another in love" he was assuming that the human heart is sinful (see Eph. 4:2).

In the book After the Baby Boomers: How Twenty- and Thirty Somethings are Shaping the Future of American Religion, Robert Wuthnow describes twenty-one to forty-five-year-olds as tinkerers. Our grandparents built. Our parents boomed. And my generation? We tinker. Of course, as Wuthnow points out, tinkering is not all bad. Those who tinker know how to improvise, specialize, pull things apart, and pull people together from a thousand different places. But tinkering also means indecision, contradiction, and instability. We are seeing a generation of young people grow up (sort of) who tinker with doctrines, tinker with churches, tinker with girlfriends and boyfriends, tinker with college majors, tinker living in and out of their parent's basement, and tinker with spiritual practices no matter how irreconcilable or divergent.

We're not consistent. We're not stable. We don't stick with anything. We aren't sure we are making the right decisions. Most of the time, we can't even make decisions. And we don't follow through. All of this means that as Christian young people we are less fruitful and less faithful than we ought to be.[10]

– Kevin DeYoung

Implied was his concession that people (yes, even Christians) will hurt one another and need to be endured, forgiven, and loved. This means you live out the truth of Scripture and demonstrate the power of the Holy Spirit by sticking with your friends and committing to them for the long haul rather than dumping them whenever they disappoint you. Commit to your friends.

What is the most sacrificial thing a Christian brother or sister has ever done toward you?

What is the most sacrificial thing you have ever done toward a Christian brother or sister?

3. Commit to a local church.
One of the most damaging practices of students and young adults is known as "church-hopping"—bouncing from church to church without committing to any. This practice is damaging because you're loosely connected to many people, rather than deeply connected to very few. More tragically, though, is that it distorts God's design for His people. God describes His New Testament people this way in the Scriptures.

---

* Facilitator: What are the differences between church-hopping and committing to a church as a member? If members of your group aren't members of a local church, gracefully encourage one another toward that.

So then you are no longer foreigners and strangers, but fellow citizens with the saints and members of God's household (Eph. 2:19).

God likens His church to a household. This carries more weight when you consider what the New Testament (at Jesus' initiative) calls Christians brothers and sisters—a spiritual family. The local manifestation of that family is the local church. So rather than church-hopping or hesitantly telling yourself, "I can't find one I completely agree with," dive in and commit to a local church. Become a member, serve, and fall in love with the family of God. Joining a local church doesn't mean you have to stay in one location forever. But you can commit to a local church now by being a member for this season in your life. Through this, God will grow in you a heart for His Church that will accompany you for life. So commit to a local church and begin experiencing all the joys that being a part of God's global family has to offer you.

Are you a member of a local church right now? If so, how can you serve in a deeper way?

If you're not a member of a local church right now, what is holding you back?

4. Commit to missions.

Have you ever turned down a missions' opportunity because you "just weren't called"? If so, you're not alone. Thousands of Christian young adults just like you say something similar each year. As a matter of fact, I said it over and over again when I was a student.

---

* Facilitator: Have you ever used the excuse "God's just not calling me"? Why is this an insufficient response to short-term mission opportunities?

But as I think about students turning down mission opportunities, I can't help but think that saying, "God's not calling me" might just be a spiritual "cop-out." Jesus' command to "make disciples of all nations" (Matt. 28:19-20) wasn't given to the spiritual elite. He gave it to each of His followers. That means He intends for every one of us to participate in that mission. So, in essence, we're all called.

Then how do you process short-term mission trips? Does Jesus' Great Commission mean you should go on every mission experience offered to you? Not exactly. It means that it's not as much an issue of calling as it is an issue of practicality. Jesus made the missionary call clear to all Christians. Therefore, it's more an issue of time and resources. Do you have the time to go? Can you reasonably raise the resources to go? Each person has their own unique circumstances, but by and large, young adults have both at their disposal. So maybe some of you reading this need to give up the excuses and actually participate in God's global mission. You can start by participating in short-term trips with your local campus or church ministry. Then you can explore long-term opportunities through a mission board. Regardless, commit to God's global mission. If not now, when?

What are you thinking in response to this mission challenge?

5. Commit to your word.

One of the most practical ways you can release the hold of reluctance and demonstrate commitment is by following through on your commitments and keeping your word.

> **But let your word 'yes' be 'yes,' and your 'no' be 'no.' Anything more than this is from the evil one (Matt. 5:37).**

In other words, when you say you're going to do something, do it. When you commit to being somewhere, be there. After signing up for something, actually show up. Follow through on your commitments.

But this discussion on following through actually leads to a caution. Remember all of the talk in this study about the barrage of opportunities available to you? Mission trips, service projects, social justice opportunities, education, and work are just a few. Just because something is available for your participation doesn't make it a biblical mandate to you personally.

You can't do everything, and you shouldn't try. In his book, *Crazy Busy*, Kevin DeYoung writes, "The people on this planet who end up doing nothing are those who never realized they couldn't do everything."[11]

To release the hold of reluctance, you must learn to balance your commitments. Wholeheartedly commit to a few things, rather than be marginally involved in many. Jesus said to keep your word. Therefore, when you do make a commitment, keep it.

When was the last time you made a commitment to someone or something and didn't follow through?

What were the ramifications for doing so?

We've made it to the end of our journey together. We hope you've been challenged in significant ways. Continue to saturate your heart with God's Word, make hard choices that break the cultural stereotypes, and make the most of every opportunity.

THIS WEEK REFLECT ON...

CLOSING RESPONSE

On a separate page or in your journal, reflect upon the following application points from this session.

- In order to commit to my work right now, I will ...
- In order to commit to my friends right now, I will ...
- In order to commit to His church right now, I will ...
- In order to commit to His mission right now, I will ...
- In order to commit to my word right now, I will ...

MAKING A CHANGE

- Think again about this statement. "Just because something is available for your participation doesn't make it a biblical mandate to you personally." Begin adjusting your schedule and commitments so you can deeply commit to a few things rather than loosely participate in many.
- Consequently, learn the value of saying both yes and no. This study has challenged you to make God-honoring commitments. As a result, release the hold of reluctance and say, "yes." On the other hand, as you commit more deeply to a few things, learn to say "no" to other things. Your commitment will grow when you guard yourself from over-commitment.

FOR FURTHER STUDY

- To aid you in taking the next steps in making the most of every opportunity, check out *Manage: Caring for all God Entrusted to Us* (available at *threadsmedia.com*).
- For a great perspective on decision-making and the will of God, consider reading *Just Do Something* by Kevin DeYoung.

END NOTES

INTRODUCTION

1. *Merriam-Webster's Collegiate Dictionary,* 11th ed., s.v. "reluctant."

SESSION 1

1. Marc Yoder, "10 Surprising Reasons Our Kids LEAVE Church," *Church Leaders,* Accessed June 6, 2014, *http://www.churchleaders.com/children/ childrens-ministry-articles/166129-marc-solas-10-surprising-reasons-our- kids-leave-church.html.*

2. The Barna Group, "Surveys Show Pastors Claim Congregants are Deeply Committed to God, but Congregants Deny It," *The Barna Group,* January 10, 2006, *https://www.barna.org/barna-update/article/5- barna-update/165-surveys-show-pastors-claim-congregants-are-deeply- committed-to-god-but-congregants-deny-it#.U5HBPtzQCbA*

3. Lee Camp, *Mere Discipleship: Radical Christianity in a Rebellious World* (Grand Rapids: Brazos Press, 2003), 27.

4. Timothy Keller, *The Prodigal God* (New York: The Penguin Group, 2008), 22.

5. John MacArthur, *The MacArthur New Testament Commentary Series: Matthew 16-23* (Chicago: Moody Press, 1988), 339.

6. Frank E. Gaebelin, ed. *The Expositor's Bible Commentary,* vol. 8, "Matthew" by D.A. Carson (Grand Rapids: Zondervan, 1984), 464.

7. Augustine, as quoted by John Piper in "Do Not Love the World," Sermon, March 10, 1984, *http://www.desiringgod.org/sermons/do-not- love-the-world*

8. Charles Swindoll, *Elijah: A Man Who Stood with God* (Nashville: Thomas Nelson, 2000), 15.

9. Dave Hunt, "God So Loved," *The Berean Call,* December 1, 2004, http:// www.thebereancall.org/content/god-so-loved

10. David Platt, "Two Simple Words: Follow Me," Sermon, January 7, 2007, *http://www.radical.net/media/series/view/44/two-simple-words-follow- me?filter=series*

11. Steven Curtis Chapman, "For the Sake of the Call" (song lyrics), accessed June 6, 2014, *http://stevencurtischapman.com/home/wp- content/uploads/For-the-Sake-of-the-Call.pdf.*

12. Adapted from David Platt, "Two Simple Words: Follow Me," Sermon, January 7, 2007, *http://www.radical.net/media/series/view/44/two- simple-words-follow-me?filter=series*

13.   J.D. Greear, *Gospel: Recovering the Power that Made Christianity Revolutionary* (Nashville: B&H, 2011), 9.

SESSION 2
1.   Mark Dever, *What is Healthy Church?* (Wheaton, IL: Crossway, 2005), 34.
2.   Wayne Grudem, *Systematic Theology* (Grand Rapids: Zondervan, 1994), 853.
3.   Matt Chandler, "Is Church Membership Biblical?" *9Marks*. June 2011. Accessed June 11, 2014. *http://www.9marks.org/journal/church-membership-biblical*.
4.   Thom Rainer, *I Am a Church Member* (Nashville: B&H, 2013), 6.
5.   Tim Chester, *You Can Change* (Wheaton, IL: Crossway, 2019), 155.
6.   Mark Dever, *What is a Healthy Church?* (Wheaton, IL: Crossway, 2005), 28-29.
7.   C. Michael Patton, *Now That I'm a Christian* (Wheaton, IL: Crossway, 2014), 122.
8.   Thabiti M. Anyabwile, *What is a Healthy Church Member?* (Wheaton, IL: Crossway, 2008), 61.
9.   Dietrich Bonhoeffer, *Life Together: Prayerbook of the Bible* (Minneapolis: Fortress Press, 1996), 33.

SESSION 3
1.   David Horner, *When Missions Shapes the Mission* (Nashville: B&H, 2011), 123.
2.   Francis Chan, *Crazy Love* (Colorado Springs: David C. Cook, 2013), 115.
3.   Donald R. Potts, "Samaria, Samaritans," in T*he Holman Illustrated Bible Dictionary*, ed. by Chad Brand, Charles Draper, and Archie England (Nashville: Holman Bible Publishers, 2003), 1436-1437.
4.   Timothy Keller, *Gospel in Life: Grace Changes Everything* (Grand Rapids: Zondervan, 2010), 109.
5.   Kevin DeYoung, "A Brief Wrap Up on the Poor and Social Justice," *The Gospel Coalition*, August 5, 2010, *http://thegospelcoalition.org/blogs/kevindeyoung/2010/08/05/a-brief-wrap-on-the-poor-and-social-justice*.
6.   John Piper, *Let the Nations Be Glad!* (Grand Rapids: Baker Publishing Group, 1993), 35.

7. "People Group Listings," *The Joshua Project*. Accessed June 9, 2014, *http://joshuaproject.net/listings/PercentEvangelical/desc/500/allctry/ allcon/allreg?&jps3=5&jps2=5#list*

8. Robert Coleman, *The Master Plan of Evangelism* (Grand Rapids: Baker Publishing Group, 2010), 109.

9. David Platt, *Radical* (Colorado Springs: Multnomah Books, 2010), 156.

SESSION 4

1. Jonathan Edwards, *The Works of Jonathan Edwards*, Vol. 1 (Edinburgh: Banner of Truth, 1976), xx-xxi.

2. Alex and Brett Harris, *Do Hard Things* (Colorado Springs: Multnomah Books, 2008), 3.

3. Thom Rainer, *The Millennials* (Nashville: B&H), 2011), 3.

4. Jonathan Edwards, *The Works of Jonathan Edwards*, Vol.1 (Edinburgh: Banner of Truth, 1976), xx-xxi.

5. J. Oswald Sanders, *Spiritual Leadership* (Chicago: Moody Bible Institute, 1967), 95.

6. Thom Rainer, *The Millennials* (Nashville: B&H, 2011), 41.

7. Donald Whitney, *Spiritual Disciplines for the Christian Life* (Colorado Springs: NavPress, 1991), 135-136.

8. John Piper, *Don't Waste Your Life* (Wheaton, IL: Crossway, 2003), 111.

9. Thom Rainer, *The Millennials* (Nashville: B&H, 2011), 108-109.

10. Kevin DeYoung, *Just Do Something* (Chicago: Moody Bible Publishers, 2009), 12.

11. Kevin DeYoung, *Crazy Busy* (Wheaton, IL: Crossway, 2013), 61.

threads
by LifeWay

An advocate of churches and people like you, Threads provides Bible studies and events designed to:

CULTIVATE COMMUNITY We need people we can call when the tire's flat or when we get the promotion. And it's those people—the day-in-day-out people—who we want to walk through life with and learn about God from.

PROVIDE DEPTH Kiddie pools are for kids. We're looking to dive in, head first, to all the hard-to-talk-about topics, tough questions, and thought-provoking Scriptures. We think this is a good thing, because we're in process. We're becoming. And who we're becoming isn't shallow.

LIFT UP RESPONSIBILITY We are committed to being responsible—doing the right things like recycling and volunteering. And we're also trying to grow in our understanding of what it means to share the gospel, serve the poor, love our neighbors, tithe, and make wise choices about our time, money, and relationships.

ENCOURAGE CONNECTION We're looking for connection with our church, our community, with somebody who's willing to walk along side us and give us a little advice here and there. We'd like opportunities to pour our lives out for others because we're willing to do that walk-along-side thing for someone else, too. We have a lot to learn from people older and younger than us. From the body of Christ.

We're glad you picked up this study. Please come by and visit us at *threadsmedia.com.*

Published by LifeWay Press®
© 2014 LifeWay Press

ISBN: 978-1-4300-3219-9
Item: 005644103

Dewey decimal classification number: 153.8
Subject heading: COMMITMENT (PSYCHOLOGY) \ CHOICE (PSYCHOLOGY) \ DECISION MAKING

Printed in the United States of America.

Young Adult Ministry Publishing
LifeWay Church Resources
One LifeWay Plaza
Nashville, Tennessee 37234-0152

We believe that the Bible has God for its author; salvation for its end; and truth, without any mixture of error, for its matter and that all Scripture is totally true and trustworthy. To review LifeWay's doctrinal guideline, please visit *www.lifeway.com/doctrinalguideline*.

Cover design by Lauren Ervin

If you find this book, either
enjoy it yourself or return to...

_____

_____

_____

_____

D1569415